ESTHER RANDALL'S

Embellishing

WITH

SILK RIBBON EMBROIDERY

I am grateful to my husband, Dan, and our blended family
of six children—my contribution (Nancy, Scot, and Esther) and
Dan's contribution (Scot, Dana, and Mike)—who for so many
years have encouraged my devotion to the art of needlework.
My special thanks are to Esther and Nancy who have
perfected their own gift for creating fine needlework.
—Esther Randall

ESTHER RANDALL'S
EMBELLISHING WITH SILK RIBBON EMBROIDERY

President and Publisher: Jeramy Lanigan Landauer
Editor: Becky Wayne Johnston
Associate Editor: Ruth Schmuff
Art Director: Lyne Neymeyer
Photographer: Lyne Neymeyer
Illustrators: Ruth Schmuff and Roxanne LeMoine
Creative Assistants: Glenda Dawson,
    Margaret Sindelar and Nicole Bratt
Prepress: Event Graphics
Printer: Quebecor Printing Book Group,
Hawkins Manufacturing Division

Flower photos by PhotoDisc.

This book is printed on acid-free paper.

ISBN: 0-9646870-2-X (h/c)
       0-9646870-1-1 (ppb)

10 9 8 7 6 5 4 3 2 1
First Edition

ESTHER RANDALL'S

Embellishing

WITH

SILK RIBBON EMBROIDERY

LANDAUER BOOKS
LANDAUER CORPORATION
CUMMING, IOWA

Contents

Introduction

Many of the projects in this exquisite collection have been designed and stitched by well-known silk ribbon embroidery designer and teacher, Esther Randall. Esther's significant contribution to advancing the art of silk ribbon embroidery is recognized worldwide.

ESTHER RANDALL

Portrait by: Gore's Country Studio

When Esther and Dan Randall purchased YLI Corporation in 1984, they had no way of knowing that YLI would eventually be known worldwide as a manufacturer of premium-quality products for the sewing industry. But the two things they did know were that Dan was an experienced business executive and Esther loved fabrics and was an experienced, creative stitcher.

Because YLI's products included silk ribbon and silk thread, it didn't take Esther long to begin embroidering with silk. At first she used familiar iron-on patterns, but soon her creativeness took her artistic ability from her own flower garden to her embroidered needlework.

She wrote in her book, *Esther's Silk Ribbon Embroidery,* "Before I begin a project I take an imaginary walk in a classic English flower garden, surrounded by an array of beautiful colors and hues. I pick an armful of flowers and mentally arrange them into a beautiful bouquet to adorn a favorite corner of my living room. This floral imagery is enhanced as I look at my basket of silk ribbons. Like the flowers in my imagined bouquet, my ribbons have all the delicate shades of color and are ready to portray in silk the exquisite shapes and colors of nature. No other stitching, I believe, can capture nature's floral beauty like silk ribbon embroidery."

Esther knew that silk ribbon embroidery was an ancient art and that through the ages it was found particularly in the Chinese, Japanese, European, and even early American cultures. Esther also knew she wanted to help bring this unique and exquisite needle art to those who love to do and those who love to view its beauty.

For many years Esther has made silk ribbon embroidery a focus of her creative needlework. She is well known for her artistic sewing, and particularly for her creative designs in silk ribbon embroidery. Her work has been featured in *McCall's Needlework; Sew Beautiful;* and *Creative Needle.* In addition, her needlework has been displayed at many trade shows.

Esther has taught silk ribbon embroidery classes and seminars throughout the United States.

Esther Randall's great love of silk ribbon embroidery, her creative expertise, and association with other leading needlework professionals have helped to associate her name with this international creative artform.

The wide range of projects also features designs from other contributing needle artists that are worked using silk ribbons for embroidery, ribbon weaving, and ribbon roses. Additional inspirations from the designers include the use of innovative materials and techniques.

OTHER CONTRIBUTERS

JOAN HUFF was inspired by Esther Randall's silk-ribbon embroidery masterpieces to combine her childhood love of embroidery with her passion for transforming ordinary eggs into dazzling jewel boxes.

The result was so spectacular that today Joan is widely-recognized in egg-ornamentation, as well as in needlework circles, for her exquisite eggshell floral artistry.

JUDITH KURTH is an accomplished designer and educator for Pfaff.

MERRY NADER'S love of embroidery and fine needlework has grown into a career of designing and teaching others the art of silk ribbon embroidery. Many of Merry's designs feature delightful new stitches and motifs inspired by her extensive collection of antique Victorian crazy quilts.

JUDY NOWICKI is a talented designer who creates numerous projects for Viking and *America Sews with Sue Hausmann.*

NORMA RESTALL'S wonderful needle art grows out of her love for her native Wales and the gardens surrounding her home in the country.

PATSY SHIELDS is a creative force in promoting silk ribbon embroidery and designs for Baby Lock.

ABOUT THE PROJECTS

All of the projects for fashions, home and holidays are accompanied by a complete how-to that features a unique, easy to use coded reference guide for stitches, materials and colors—a first for silk ribbon enthusiasts. (See How To Use This Book.)

MATERIALS

FABRIC
2- 7x9-inch (18x23-cm) pieces of light mauve wool crepe

EMBROIDERY THREAD
YLI 601 fine metallic thread (**A**): Gold (GLD)
Kanagawa 1000 denier silk embroidery thread (**B**) in each

of the following colors: light blue (105), light yellow (141), and eggplant (819)
Kanagawa 380 denier silk embroidery thread (**C**) in: light green (31)

SILK EMBROIDERY RIBBON
5-yard (4.5m) reel of YLI 7-mm silk embroidery ribbon (**D**) in each of the following colors: green (32), rose (127), medium rose (128), and antique violet (178)
5-yard (4.5m) reel of YLI 4-mm silk embroidery ribbon (**E**) in each of the following colors: spring green (18), lavender (101), medium rose (128), and teal (133)
5-yard (4.5m) reel of YLI 2-mm silk embroidery ribbon (**F**) in: light teal (131)

ADDITIONAL MATERIALS
AK Designs seed beads: light blue (11/112A)
Beading monocord
Beading needle - No. 10
Chenille needle - No. 24
Crewel needle - No. 7
Dresser set with removable inserts

HOW TO USE THIS BOOK

You'll find that a special feature of the complete how-to instructions for each project is the easy-to-use coded reference guide for stitches, materials, and colors.

Begin by referring to the embroidery pattern that shows the design and position of the stitches. As shown here, the pattern is drawn in full detail with an accompanying code. The code has three elements: a number in a circle, a capital letter, and a number or series of numbers.

The first element— a number in a circle— indicates the stitch that you will use to make a flower, leaf, or stem.

Note: All the stitches used in a project are identified in the STITCHES box located on the same page as the embroidery pattern. (The Step-by-Step Guide to the Stitches begins on page 126.)

The second element—a capital letter— denotes the thread or ribbon used for that particular stitch.

The third and final element— a number or series of numbers— indicates the ribbon or thread color.

Note: The ribbons and colors are identified in the MATERIALS list that appears with the project.

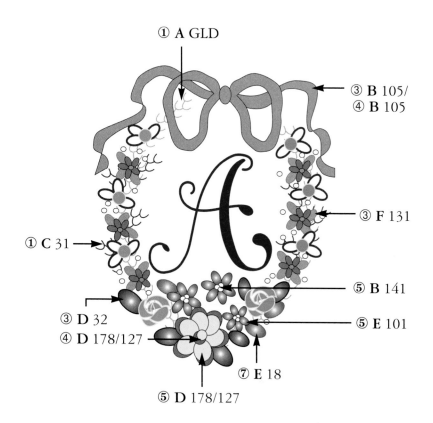

① A GLD
③ B 105/
④ B 105
③ F 131
① C 31
⑤ B 141
③ D 32
④ D 178/127
⑤ E 101
⑦ E 18
⑤ D 178/127

S T I T C H E S
① Fern Stitch *(page 129)*
② Straight Stitch *(page 135)*
③ Stem Stitch *(page 134)*
④ French Knot Stitch *(page 130)*
⑤ Japanese Ribbon Stitch *(page 131)*
⑥ Straight Stitch Rose *(page 141)*
⑦ Lazy Daisy Stitch *(page 132)*

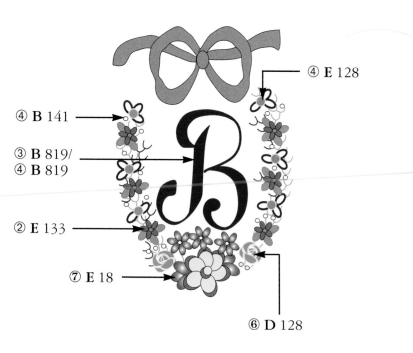

④ E 128
④ B 141
③ B 819/
④ B 819
② E 133
⑦ E 18
⑥ D 128

shown 75% of actual finished size

9

TIPS AND TECHNIQUES FOR GETTING STARTED

USING SILK RIBBON

Silk ribbon embroidery is a skill. With patience and practice it quickly becomes second nature and is easily completed. Because of the ribbon size, there are fewer stitches necessary, and they cover more space than ordinary embroidery thread. Five widths of ribbon can be used—2mm (1⁄16"), 4mm (1⁄8"), 7mm (1⁄4"), 13mm (1⁄2"), or 32 mm (1 1⁄4")—depending upon the scale of the work, desired texture, and the designer's preference.

As you stitch with silk ribbon, watch the colors and textures come alive under your fingers. It is important that you handle and lay the ribbon properly to control its curling—either adding or eliminating the curling—to give each stitch its natural appearance. Silk ribbon is flat, not round like threads and yarns and should be kept flat whenever possible. Keep the ribbon flat and smooth on the back of the stitchery, since a twist in the ribbon on the wrong side of the stitchery will affect the embroidery on the front.

When first learning silk ribbon embroidery, a laying tool is helpful—use it to smooth or to fluff the ribbon, or to set the stitch. A laying tool can be something as simple as a long needle, such as a stole needle or doll-making needle. A trolley needle or even a large, oval-head corsage pin works well to smooth out the stitch and "lift" the ribbon to get the desired look. As you develop more skill, your thumb or index finger will become a more natural laying tool. Remember, the objective of using a laying tool is to guide the ribbon from the front of your work and to keep the full width of the ribbon, so that your combined stitches look like real flowers. Have the stitch properly formed before the stitch is completed; do not try to overly adjust the embroidery once complete.

No matter what stitch or size of ribbon, the process is the same. The importance of keeping the ribbon flat is the same. Bring the ribbon through the fabric holding it gently against the fabric. Keeping the ribbon flat with a loose tension allows the embroidery stitches to remain full and not lose their desired shape. Allow the ribbon to follow its natural tendency to flow toward the next point of the stitch. Bring the needle to the wrong side of the fabric. Again, lay the ribbon flat on the wrong side, preparing for the next stitch. Bring the needle up. Hold the ribbon close to the fabric with your thumb and forefinger and gently twist the ribbon as it comes through the fabric to align the ribbon.

Silk ribbon that has been distorted can be easily brought back to life. Dampen the ribbon at the damaged point. Using the thumb and forefinger of your left hand, hold the ribbon just below the damaged point. With your right hand hold the ribbon just above the damaged point. Stroke and flatten the ribbon until it looks like new. Even a small 3" scrap can be salvaged for a French knot flower center.

Note: Dampening the silk ribbon will allow the fibers to expand as they dry, bringing back the full width of the ribbon.

USING HOOPS

An embroidery hoop helps keep your needlework, especially the ribbon, smooth. Use a hoop that is easy to handle. Round, wooden hoops ⅜" or 8mm wide with a screw adjustment for tension work best. Look for a hardwood, smooth finish hoop which will not mar your silk ribbon embroidery. A small hoop allows for more control when using your thumb and forefinger to lay the ribbon. The center of the design is easily reached.

When working on a large project, try using a hoop stand to hold the embroidery hoop. It frees both hands and keeps the embroidery steady.

SELECTING NEEDLES

A variety of needles are important in silk ribbon embroidery. The size of the ribbon and the fabric you are stitching on will determine the needle choice.

SELECTING FABRICS

Because silk is a natural fiber, it will be compatible with other natural fibers, such as wool, linen, cotton, and silk fabrics. However, all fabrics can be used. Beautiful counted work can be done on Aida cloth. Just try to match the size weave in the fabric with the size ribbon you are using.

When planning to stitch with dark or bright-colored ribbons, check to see if they will show through the selected fabric. If so, it is necessary to add a backing fabric. Some projects will need a backing fabric to give the fabric more stability. Fabrics that work best as backing are: China silk, silk organza, and soft cottons.

THREADING THE NEEDLE

Cut off a 14-inch piece of ribbon diagonally with small sharp embroidery scissors. (A longer piece of ribbon is difficult to manage and will soon appear damaged because of the many times it is pulled through the fabric.) Slip the ribbon's diagonal point through the needle's eye and pull it through.

Beginning Knots/Tying Knots

With each new length of ribbon, make sure it is securely attached to the underside of the fabric so it will not pull through as you begin your stitches.

A regular sewing knot is used as a beginning knot, when the embroidered item gets lots of use, or when the underside of the completed project is covered, such as framed embroidery. Simply tie a knot at the end of the ribbon. Slide it to the very end and pull tight. Clip the excess ribbon close to the knot.

Ending Knots

Hold the embroidery with the underside facing you. Apply pressure to the completed stitches from the right side of the fabric with the forefinger of your left hand. Take a small stitch on the underside of the stitchery beneath a petal or leaf. With the needle still on the underside of the fabric, pierce the center of the ribbon approximately ⅛" from the fabric. Pull secure and clip the tail.

Choosing a Design

As you select a pattern for your silk ribbon embroidery, look at the pattern in terms of the final appearance you can achieve with silk ribbon. Regular press-on patterns can be used, but the silk ribbon will add a dimension of realism to the completed embroidery that cannot be achieved with regular embroidery thread. When stitching over a printed design—whether a press-on design or one you have drawn yourself—remember to stitch just outside the lines so that they do not show through.

As you become more familiar with the various embroidery stitches that can be sewn with silk ribbon, you will plan and design your own patterns. Your creative style and artistic ability will emerge as you select ribbon color, ribbon size, and appropriate stitches to create your own floral pictures.

Care

Silk ribbon embroidery is meant to be enjoyed for many years. Do not be afraid to use it. Pure silk ribbon from YLI will not run when washed or dried. As with many threads, fabrics and yarns, certain dark or bright colors may bleed—particularly dark blues or reds. It is advisable to set these colors to the ribbon before stitching.

Note: To set the colors in ribbon, combine a gallon of warm water, .5 ounces of salt and .5 ounces of vinegar. Submerge ribbon in this mixture until water cools. Remove ribbon and rinse under cold water. Allow to dry. Press ribbon as necessary.

NEEDLES

Beading

Size 10 Use for embellishing ribbon embroidery with beads or sequins.

Betweens

Size 10 Use for quilting with 601 metallic thread. Appliqúe with size 50 or 100 silk thread.

Chenille (large oval eye, sharp point) Use for tightly-woven fabrics, taffeta, moire, velvet.

Size 26 2mm or 4mm ribbon

Size 24 7mm ribbon

Size 18 13mm ribbon

Size 13 32mm ribbon, organdy ribbon, or laying tool

Darners

Size 7 Use for smocking with 2mm or 4mm ribbon.

Embroidery Crewel (oval eye, sharp point)

Size 8 2mm ribbon or 380 denier silk thread

Size 7 4mm ribbon

Milliner's

Size 7 Use for embroidery with 1000 denier silk thread; longer length is helpful when making bullion stitches and French knots.

Sharps

Size 7 Use for embroidery with 1000 denier silk thread.

Tapestry (large oval eye, blunt point) Use for even-weave fabrics and weaving stitches where needle passes between fabric and previous stitching.

Size 26 2mm or 4mm ribbon

Size 24 7mm ribbon

PLAIN *and* FANCY

Jackets, Vests, Collars and Cuffs

Discover how easily festive fashions get all dressed up with the simple addition of silk ribbon embroidery embellishments.

Whether you use purchased ready-mades or your favorite garment pattern, the results are fast—but fabulous!

On the following pages you'll find silk ribbon embroidery inspirations you can make for yourself, family or friends for all those special seasons of your life.

PARTY DRESS

Choose a palette of silk ribbons in complimentary colors to transform a plain puffed-sleeve party dress into a floral masterpiece with a scattering of embroidery embellishments. For your "canvas" begin with a purchased dress or make one from your favorite pattern. (For the pattern Esther used, see Sources.) Following the pattern with the coded reference for stitches, materials, and colors, work the embroidery.

MATERIALS

FABRIC
Deep green Dupioni 100% handwoven silk (See Sources.)

SILK EMBROIDERY RIBBON
5-yard (4.5m) reel of YLI 7-mm silk embroidery ribbon (**D**) in the following colors: pink (8), green (31), medium blue (82), burgundy (84), eggplant (85), fuchsia (146), and antique mauve (179)

ADDITIONAL MATERIALS
Chenille needle –No. 24, No. 26

STITCHES
① Japanese Ribbon Stitch
   (*page 131*)
② French Knot Stitch
   (*page 130*)
③ Under-folded Loop Stitch
   (*page 136*)

① D 8

③ D 146

① D 85

② D 82

① D 84

② D 8

③ D 179

① D 85

② D 146

① D 31

① D 82

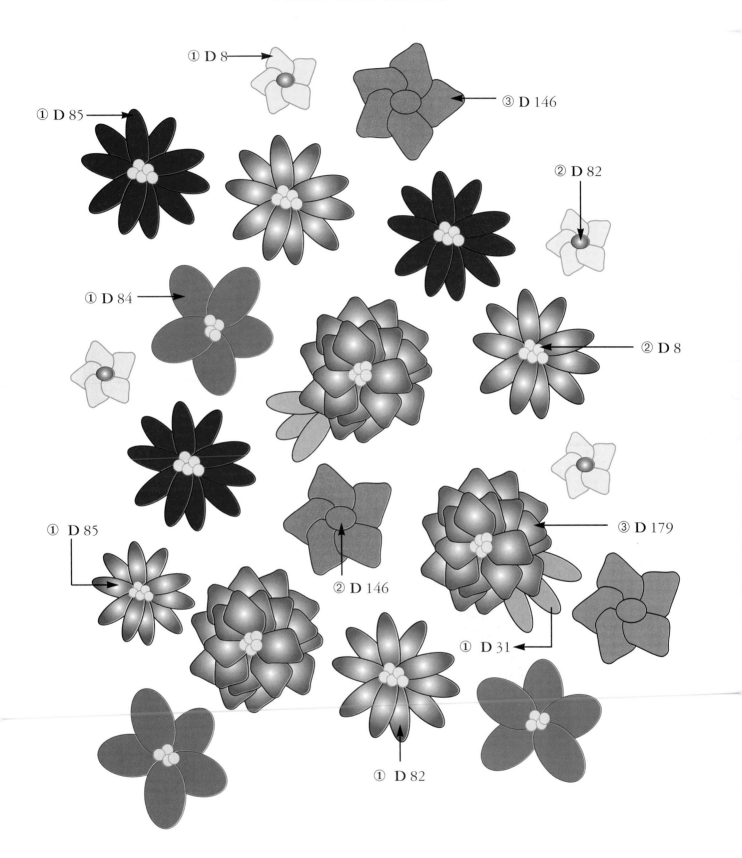

shown at 80% actual finished size

GIRL'S VELVET COAT

Discover how easy it is to add a little holiday spirit to almost anything—even a purchased coat! When embellished with festive seasonal accents on the buttons, collar and cuffs, a velvet coat becomes the perfect complement to a pretty party dress. Add silk ribbon poinsettia blooms with stems and leaves to the picot-lace trimmed collar and cuffs. Top it all off by embroidering a single poinsettia bloom for each of the buttons.

With silk ribbon, embroider directly on the collar and cuffs of the coat, working between the velvet and the lining as necessary.

For the buttons, stitch individual blooms on scraps of velvet. Wrap each onto a covered-button form to create unique holiday-inspired buttons for the coat.

MATERIALS

FABRIC
Dark green velvet coat

EMBROIDERY THREAD
Kanagawa 1000 denier silk
    embroidery thread (**B**) in:
    spring green (165)

SILK EMBROIDERY RIBBON
5-yard (4.5m) reel of YLI 7-mm
    silk embroidery ribbon (**D**) in the
    following colors: medium avocado
    (20), and cranberry (49)

5-yard (4.5m) reel of YLI 4-mm
    silk embroidery ribbon (**E**) in the
    following colors: yellow (14), and
    cranberry (49)

ADDITIONAL MATERIALS
Covered button forms
Chenille needle - No. 24, No. 26

STITCHES
① Japanese Ribbon Stitch
    (page 131)
② French Knot Stitch
    (page 130)
③ Chain Stitch *(page 127)*

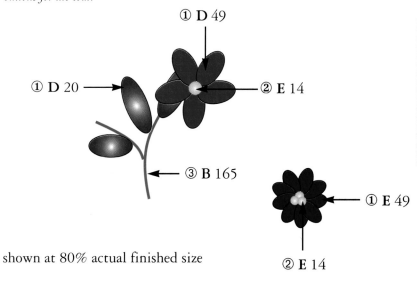

shown at 80% actual finished size

GARDEN FLOWERS DRESS

For a finishing touch, accent the smocked bodice on a little girl's dress with forever-fresh flowers. Following the pattern with the coded reference for stitches, materials, and colors work the embroidery. Or, use your imagination and scraps of silk ribbon to plant your own garden of favorite flowers. As you stitch, adjust the proportions of the petals, stems and leaves to fit the size of the dress you are embellishing. (Note: work a French knot in the tip of each petal to preserve the flower shapes during washing.)

Esther Randall delights in making and embellishing dresses with silk ribbon embroidery for her granddaughters. As Esther recalls fondly, "The reward for my efforts is having a child say, as our Ashley did several years ago, 'Now, mother, when I grow out of this dress, do not give it away. I want to save it for when I have a little girl of my own.' I thought that was pretty special!"

MATERIALS

FABRIC
Smocked fabric for bodice of girl's
dress (For the dress pattern shown
here, see Sources.)

EMBROIDERY THREAD
Kanagawa 1000 denier silk
embroidery thread (B) in each of
the following colors: green (31),
and spring green (165)

SILK EMBROIDERY RIBBON
5-yard (4.5m) reel of YLI 7-mm
silk embroidery ribbon (D) in
each of the following colors:
medium green (32), and pink (68)
5-yard (4.5m) reel of YLI 4-mm
silk embroidery ribbon (E) in:
lavender (22), medium green
(32), peach (39), dark rose (114),
light blue (125), and blue (126)

ADDITIONAL MATERIALS
Chenille needle – No. 24, No. 26
Milliner's needle – No. 7

STITCHES
① Japanese Ribbon Stitch
   (page 131)
② Chain Stitch (page 127)
③ Lazy Daisy Stitch
   (page 132)
④ French Knot Stitch
   (page 130)
⑤ Stem Stitch (page 134)
⑥ Straight Stitch (page 135)
⑦ Looped Petal Stitch
   (page 132)

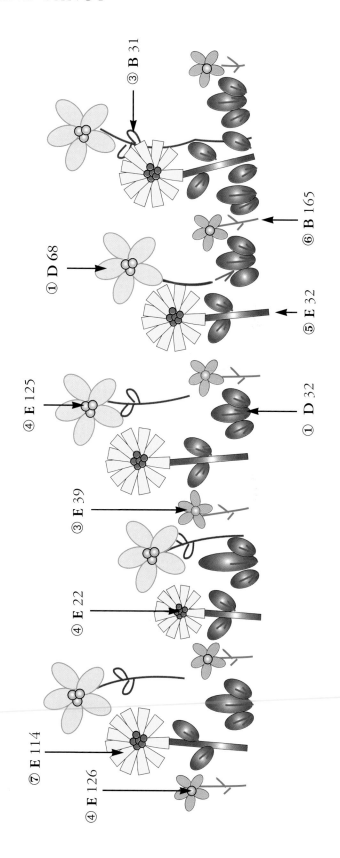

③ B 31
⑥ B 165
① D 68
⑤ E 32
④ E 125
① D 32
③ E 39
④ E 22
⑦ E 114
④ E 126

shown 70 % actual finished size

21

PIECED VEST

Surround yourself with flowers when you embellish a vest with a few of your favorite blooms. Begin by weaving silk ribbons and threads into strips of laces and eyelets.

Then strip-piece them, interspersed with scraps of silk broadcloth, linen, and cotton beading fabric.

Embellish the resulting pieced-fabric combination with embroidered flowers using a variety of stitches including the Japanese ribbon stitch and the spiral rose. Add as many floral motifs as desired, and then make the vest from your favorite purchased pattern. (For the pattern Esther used, see Sources.)

For serious stitchers like Esther, a pieced vest provides ample opportunity for putting all those leftover bits and pieces of silk ribbon and thread to good use!

MATERIALS

FABRIC
Assorted laces and eyelets
Linen and cotton beading fabric
Silk broadcloth for backing

SILK EMBROIDERY RIBBON
5-yard (4.5m) reel of YLI 7-mm
    silk embroidery ribbon (**D**) in:
    green (31)
5-yard (4.5m) reel of YLI 4-mm
    silk embroidery ribbon (**E**) in:
    yellow (13), green (18),
    medium green (31), peach (39),
    rose (128)

ADDITIONAL MATERIALS
Chenille needle - No. 24, No. 26

STITCHES

① Japanese Ribbon Stitch *(page 131)*
② Chain Stitch *(page 127)*
③ Lazy Daisy Stitch *(page 132)*
④ French Knot Stitch *(page 130)*
⑤ Straight Stitch *(page 135)*
⑥ Under-folded Loop Stitch *(page 136)*
⑦ Spiral Rose *(page 140)*

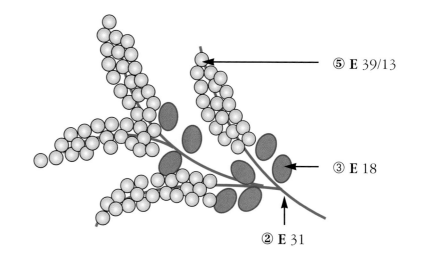

⑤ **E** 39/13

③ **E** 18

② **E** 31

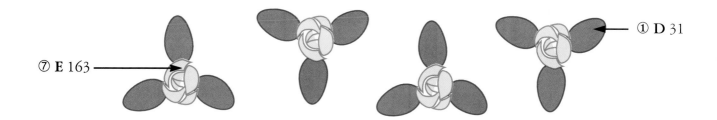

⑦ **E** 163

① **D** 31

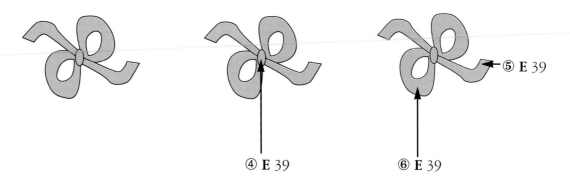

④ **E** 39

⑥ **E** 39

⑤ **E** 39

shown actual finished size

CRAZY QUILT VEST

The revival of silk ribbon embroidery and interest in all things Victorian go hand-in-hand when combined on an elegant crazy-quilted vest embellished with more than a dozen delightful stitches. The embroidery embellishments featured here are shown in greater detail on the vest panel diagrams you'll find on the following pages.

Since every crazy-quilted piece will vary, use Esther's intricately-detailed work of art as an inspiration for your own masterpiece!

When she began piecing together scraps of fabrics for her crazy patch, Esther Randall was delighted to finally find a use for a closetful of—you guessed it—her husband's outdated neckties! In addition to adding texture and vivid color, many of these relics sport small motifs that lend themselves to outlining. The added embellishment contributes even more to the desired dimensional effect of the completed crazy patch.

Just like adding pieces to a jigsaw puzzle, once you begin assembling a variety of fabric scraps into a crazy patch you might find yourself getting caught up in the challenge of fitting in "just one more piece" until you suddenly have enough for several vests or even an entire quilt!

Regardless of the size of your finished piece, the basic assembly technique remains the same.

Since crazy quilts rarely have a layer of batting, a foundation fabric is used to give the finished piece stability. The scraps of fabric are first pinned in place and then hand- or machine-pieced to the foundation fabric.

For the foundation, select a lightweight fabric such as muslin, sheeting, or batiste. Cut the foundation fabric roughly the size of what you will need for your desired project. This will eliminate the temptation to keep on piecing forever!

After you've gathered up scraps of a variety of fabrics—lightweight wools, silks, satins, and even silk neckties—choose one small piece to begin the crazy patch.

Center this first piece on the foundation fabric right side up and pin it in place. Matching one raw edge, place a second piece wrong side up over the first piece and pin or baste in place through both pieces and the foundation. Machine stitch ¼ inch (6 mm) from the matching raw edges of the fabrics.

Fold the second piece to the right side and press the seam flat. You will need to trim the two edges of the second piece on either side of the seam so that they line up with the corresponding edges of the first piece to form a straight line.

Your third piece will be added the same way—along one of the straight edges formed by the first two pieces. Continue adding pieces, work from the center out until you have completely covered the foundation fabric with crazy patches.

Before you begin the embroidery embellishments, Esther suggests you lay the pattern pieces for your vest panels on the foundation fabric and trace lightly around them with a water-soluble marking pen. When you work the embroidery, stitch only to the pattern outlines, so that your completed embroidery does not extend into the seam allowances to protect the embroidery from getting clipped or cut during the actual vest construction.

Now you are ready to embellish the seams with stitches like the feather, fern, fishbone, herringbone, and buttonhole. Decorate the center of each patch with a floral motif like the spiral rose or clusters of French knots, and then outline the small motifs on the fabrics with stem or straight stitches, as desired.

Use a vest pattern (see Sources) to construct the vest panels from the crazy-pieced foundation.

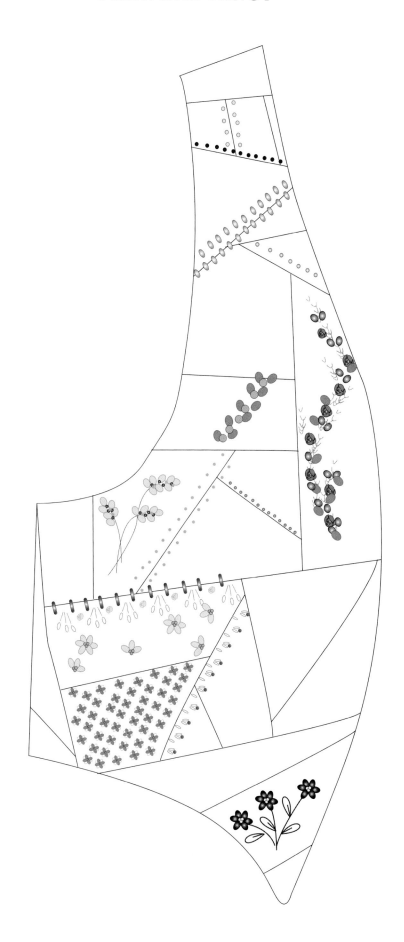

shown at 35% actual finished size

SOFT COMFORTS

A Floral Bouquet of Quilted Afghans and Pillows

At home in just about any setting, afghans and pillows lend polished elegance when embellished with silk ribbon embroidery.

The stunning center medallion afghan shown here is accompanied by another equally impressive fringed afghan featuring six floral motifs you can mix and match on the stitching blocks as desired. After the stitching was completed on the ready-made afghans by Charles Craft, both were uniquely quilted with a layer of batting and a satin background lining for additional soft comfort.

To complement the embellished afghans, a trio of pillows each with its own floral fantasy is included in three popular shapes—round, rectangular, and square—for greater decorative impact when grouped.

CENTER MEDALLION AFGHAN

The spectacular silk ribbon embroidery in the center of this afghan is surprisingly simple to re-create.

It is composed of four identical segments that form a circle. Since each segment is worked from the diagram shown in detail on the following page, once you've completed the first "slice of the pie," you'll only need to stitch three more slices!

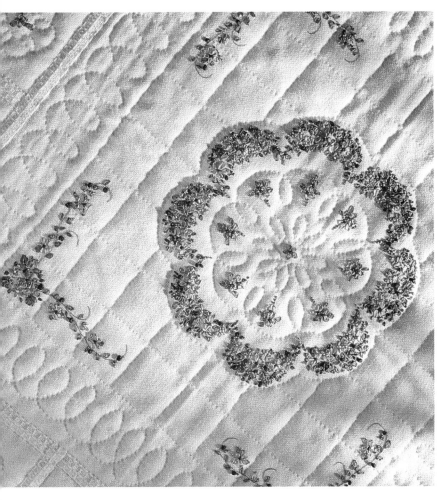

MATERIALS

FABRIC
Charles Craft precut ivory afghan

EMBROIDERY THREAD
Kanagawa 1000 denier silk
  embroidery thread (**B**) in:
  green (165)

SILK EMBROIDERY RIBBON
5-yard (4.5m) reel of YLI 7-mm
  silk embroidery ribbon (**D**) in
  each of the following colors:
  light pink (7), medium green
  (32), green (33), light blue
  (125), rose (127), deep rose
  (129), old rose (163),
  and mauve (178)
5-yard (4.5m) reel of YLI 4-mm
  silk embroidery ribbon (**E**) in
  each of the following colors:
  light yellow (14), peach (39),
  and old rose (163)

ADDITIONAL MATERIALS
Crewel needle - No. 18

Lightly trace a 13.5" (34 cm) diameter circle in the center of your afghan fabric, dividing it into eight equal sections. Following the pattern with the coded reference for stitches, materials, and colors, begin working the silk ribbon embroidery, nibbling away at stitching your eight segments one quarter at a time. Work the corner motifs, adding a border of a single floral motif in evenly-spaced blocks along the edges of the afghan.

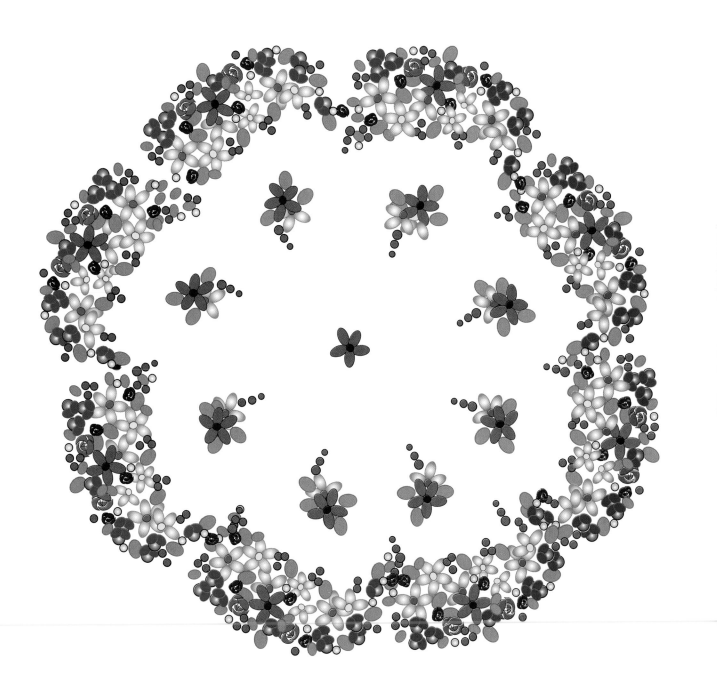

shown at 50% actual finished size

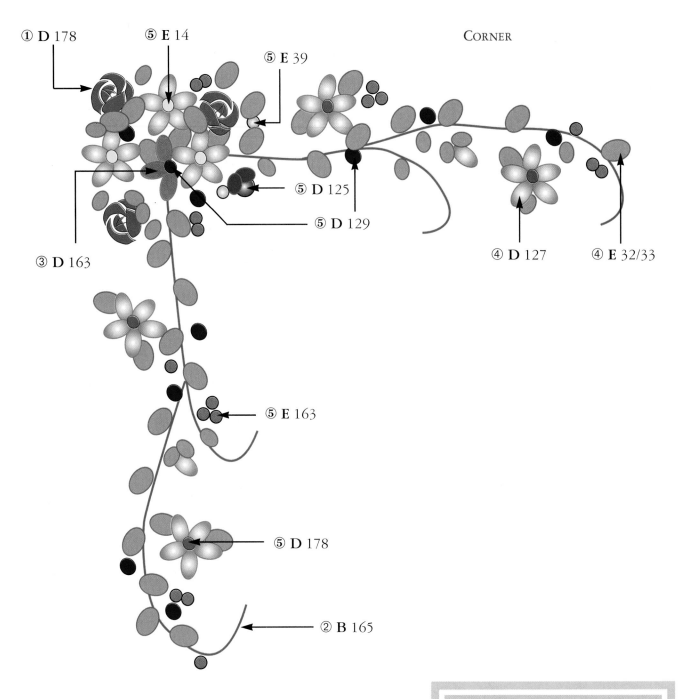

① **D** 178

⑤ **E** 14

⑤ **E** 39

⑤ **D** 125

⑤ **D** 129

③ **D** 163

④ **D** 127

④ **E** 32/33

⑤ **E** 163

⑤ **D** 178

② **B** 165

STITCHES
① Lazy Daisy and Straight Stitch
  Rose *(page 139)*
② Stem Stitch *(page 134)*
③ Japanese Ribbon Stitch
  (page 131)
④ Lazy Daisy Stitch *(page 132)*
⑤ French Knot Stitch
  (page 130)

shown at 80% actual finished size

ONE QUARTER OF MEDALLION

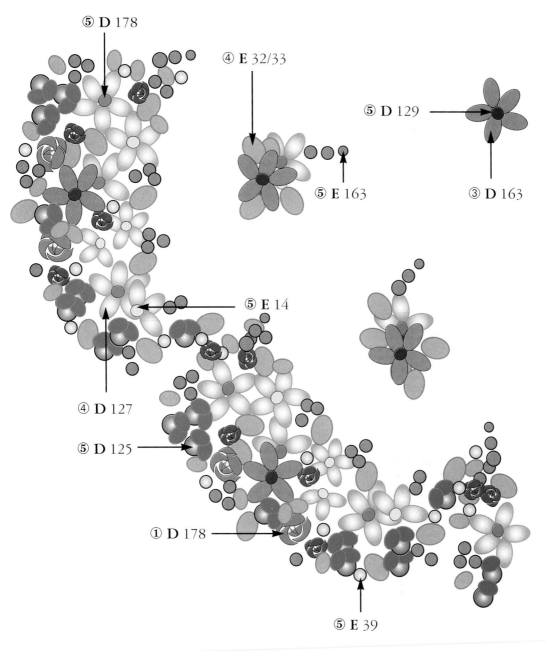

⑤ D 178

④ E 32/33

⑤ D 129

⑤ E 163

③ D 163

⑤ E 14

④ D 127

⑤ D 125

① D 178

⑤ E 39

A trademark of Esther's creative needle is giving the stitched leaves a more realistic look by threading both shades of green ribbon in the needle at the same time and stitching with them as one.

Esther also found another creative way to give the completed afghan more polish by backing it with a thin layer of quilt batting sandwiched between the afghan top and a soft lining fabric. Thus, all the ribbon ends are encased securely between the layers.

Quilt as much as desired, using your favorite quilt pattern.

shown at 80% actual finished size

FLORAL MOTIFS AFGHAN QUILT

Choose from a half dozen miniature floral motifs to embroider a garden of silk flowers on a precut ivory afghan.

Use the six motifs in any combination to fill the squares on your afghan. For a coordinated decorating theme, you might *want to purchase an additional afghan and from it cut one strip of blocks to make a runner for the dresser. Cut the remaining blocks apart to create an assortment of floral-embellished throw pillows.*

After Esther completed the stitching and created her unique afghan-quilt, she had another inspiration for finishing it in style.

Since her scrap basket was a treasury of leftover lengths of silk ribbon, Esther combined them into bundles of variegated colors and cut them into lengths suitable for tying into a colorful border fringe.

MATERIALS

FABRIC
Charles Craft precut ivory afghan

EMBROIDERY THREAD
Kanagawa 1000 denier silk embroidery thread (**B**) in: blue (34), bright green (133), spring green (165), and antique mauve (190)

SILK EMBROIDERY RIBBON
5-yard (4.5m) reel of YLI 7-mm silk embroidery ribbon (**D**) in each of the following colors: light green (31), green (33), lavender (101), rose (128), light yellow (156), and old rose (163)

5-yard (4.5m) reel of YLI 4-mm silk embroidery ribbon (**E**) in each of the following colors: blue (11), light yellow (14), green (33), beige (35), peach (39), gold (53), spring green (60), turquoise (81), deep blue (82), lavender (101), purple (102), periwinkle (117), dark periwinkle (118), and rose (128)

5-yard (4.5m) reel of YLI 13-mm silk embroidery ribbon (**G**) in each of the following colors: light yellow (13), and pink (68)

ADDITIONAL MATERIALS
Crewel needle - No. 18

STITCHES
① Straight Stitch Rose
   (page 141)
② Stem Stitch *(page 134)*
③ Japanese Ribbon Stitch
   (page 131)
④ Lazy Daisy Stitch *(page 132)*
⑤ French Knot Stitch
   (page 130)
⑥ Looped Petal Stitch
   (page 132)
⑦ Couching Stitch *(page 127)*
⑧ Straight Stitch *(page 135)*
⑨ Satin Stitch *(page 134)*
⑩ Lazy Daisy and Straight
   Stitch Rose *(page 139)*

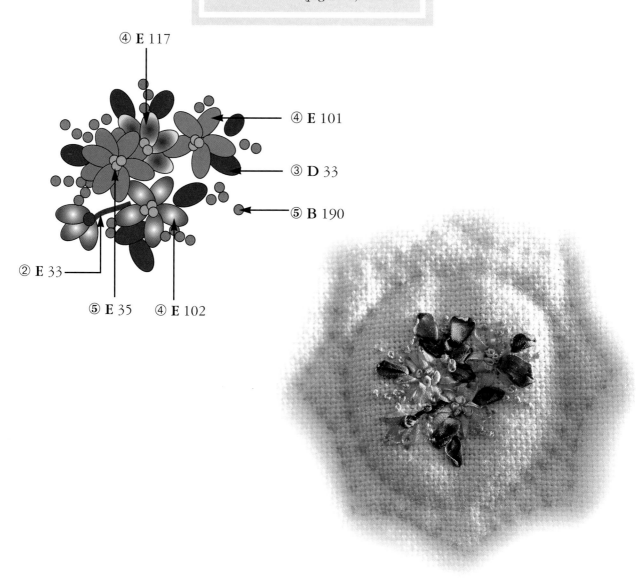

④ **E** 117

④ **E** 101

③ **D** 33

⑤ **B** 190

② **E** 33

⑤ **E** 35   ④ **E** 102

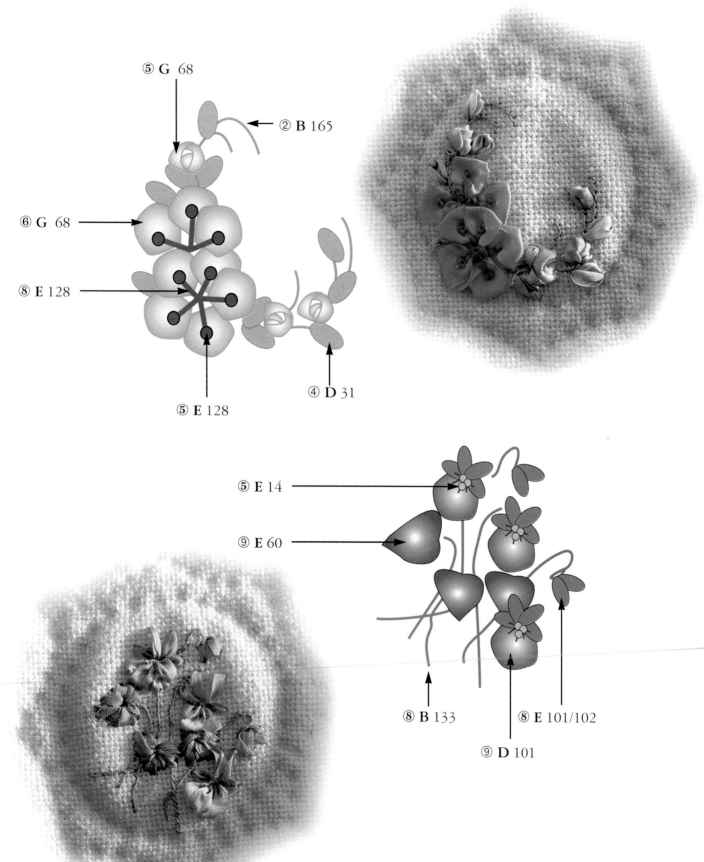

⑤ **G** 68

② **B** 165

⑥ **G** 68

⑧ **E** 128

⑤ **E** 128

④ **D** 31

⑤ **E** 14

⑨ **E** 60

⑧ **B** 133

⑨ **D** 101

⑧ **E** 101/102

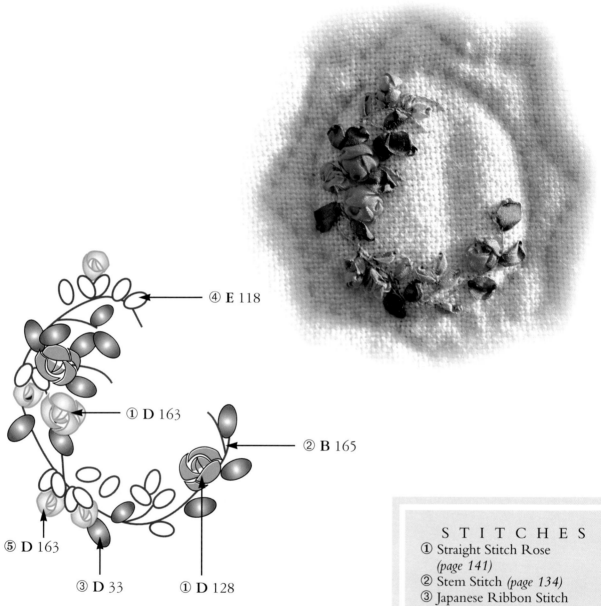

④ **E** 118

① **D** 163

② **B** 165

⑤ **D** 163

③ **D** 33

① **D** 128

STITCHES
① Straight Stitch Rose
   (page 141)
② Stem Stitch *(page 134)*
③ Japanese Ribbon Stitch
   (page 131)
④ Lazy Daisy Stitch *(page 132)*
⑤ French Knot Stitch
   (page 130)
⑥ Looped Petal Stitch
   (page 132)
⑦ Couching Stitch *(page 127)*
⑧ Straight Stitch *(page 135)*
⑨ Satin Stitch *(page 134)*
⑩ Lazy Daisy and Straight
   Stitch Rose *(page 139)*

shown at actual finished size

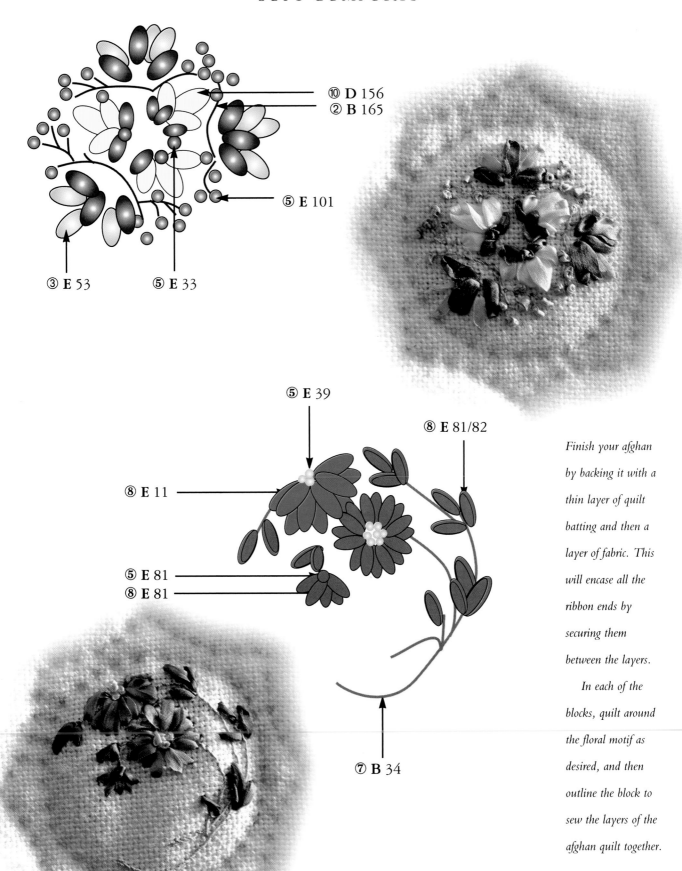

⑩ **D** 156
② **B** 165

⑤ **E** 101

③ **E** 53

⑤ **E** 33

⑤ **E** 39

⑧ **E** 81/82

⑧ **E** 11

⑤ **E** 81
⑧ **E** 81

⑦ **B** 34

Finish your afghan by backing it with a thin layer of quilt batting and then a layer of fabric. This will encase all the ribbon ends by securing them between the layers.

In each of the blocks, quilt around the floral motif as desired, and then outline the block to sew the layers of the afghan quilt together.

shown at actual finished size

PILLOW TRIO

This garden of floral delights will be a triple treat when you stitch up all three of the motifs featured on the cluster of pillows shown here. Following the pattern with the coded reference for stitches, materials, and colors, work the embroidery. Finish each pillow with piping, lace, and a ruffle in colors to match your decor.

To make softly-shaded delphiniums for the rectangular pillow, mix combinations of two colors of ribbon in your needle and stitch with them as one. Keep one ribbon consistent in both combinations.

Use the lighter pair for the French knots at the top of the flower and the deeper pair for working the French knots at the bottom of the flower.

MATERIALS

FABRIC
1–19x19-inch (48x48-cm) piece of ivory 100% wool challis for round pillow, 1–16x22-inch (40.5x56-cm) piece for rectangular pillow, and 1–17x17-inch (43x43-cm) piece for square pillow

EMBROIDERY THREAD
Kanagawa 1000 denier silk embroidery thread (**B**) in each of the following colors: spring green (31), bright green (133), and olive green (156)

SILK EMBROIDERY RIBBON
5-yard (4.5m) reel of YLI 7-mm silk embroidery ribbon (**D**) in each of the following colors: light pink (7), light sage green (31), light lavender (100), lavender (101), purple (102) rose (127), pale yellow (156), and old rose (163)

5-yard (4.5m) reel of YLI 4-mm silk embroidery ribbon (**E**) in each of the following colors: pink (8), aqua (10), light yellow (14), dark green (20), very dark green (21), ecru (34), slate blue (44), dark slate blue (46), light emerald green (60), emerald green (61), eggplant (85), light lavender (100), lavender (101), and light blue (126)

ADDITIONAL MATERIALS
Tapestry needle – No. 24, No. 26
Milliner's needle – No. 7

QUICK-AND-EASY EMBELLISHING
WITH PRE-FINISHED MATERIALS

With exciting new developments in pre-finished materials, discover how much of your creative time can be spent on the pleasures of stitching without the bother and expense of finishing. Since silk ribbon embroidery embellishments are not limited to evenweave materials, you can stitch on just about any smooth or textured fabric surface—even smocking!

To inspire you, we've gathered several of the projects featured in this book that are quick and easy thanks to pre-finished materials like the oval lidded box, the ceramic jar, and the exquisite jeweled egg box, below. Once you start exploring the possibilities, let your imagination be your guide. You may even discover something more exotic to stitch on than the embellished eggs shown here! (For Joan Huff's exquisite eggshell floral artistry, see page 96.)

Listed here are a number of quick and easy applications that are readily available in your local needlework shop or craft store.

AFGHANS

APRONS

BOOKMARKS

CERAMIC JARS

CLOCK INSERTS

COASTERS

CRYSTAL JARS

LIDDED BOXES

PILLOWS

PINS

PLACE MATS

TABLECLOTHS

TABLE RUNNERS

TOTE BAGS

TRAY INSERTS

STITCHING BANDS

VESTS

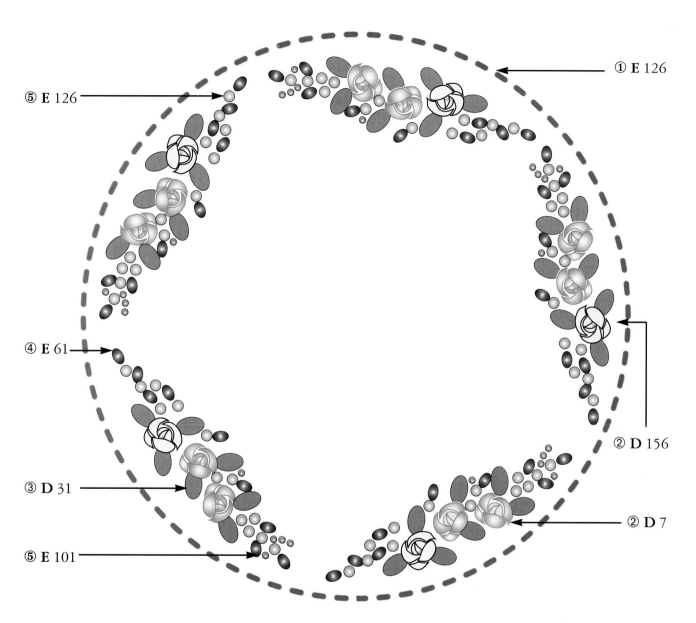

① **E** 126

⑤ **E** 126

④ **E** 61

③ **D** 31

⑤ **E** 101

② **D** 156

② **D** 7

shown at 70% actual finished size

STITCHES

① Running Stitch *(page 133)*
② Straight Stitch Rose
   (page 141)
③ Japanese Ribbon Stitch
   (page 131)
④ Lazy Daisy Stitch *(page 132)*
⑤ French Knot Stitch
   (page 130)

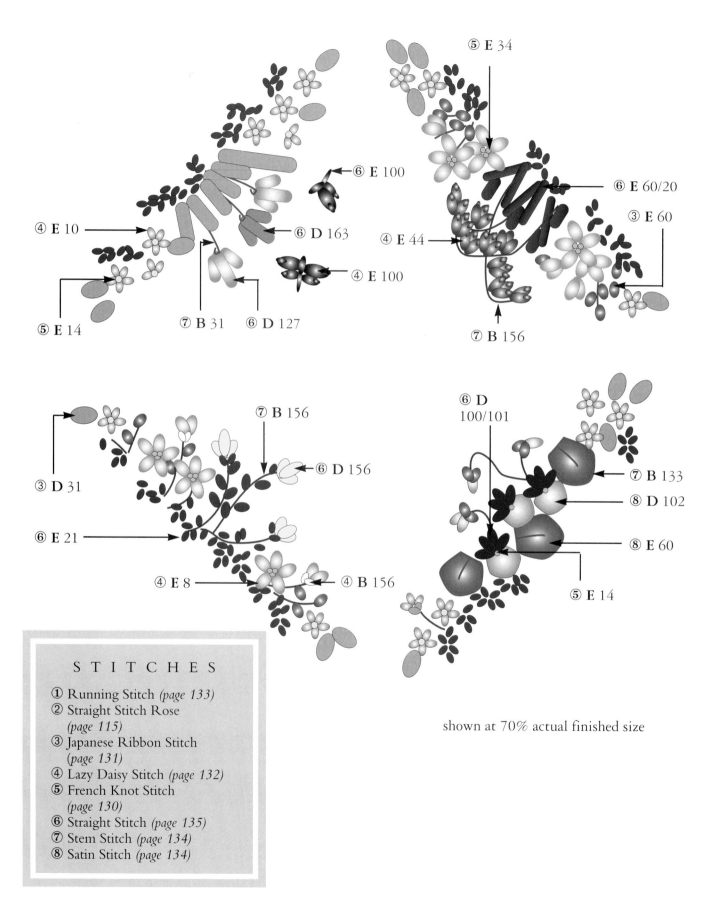

⑤ **E** 34

⑥ **E** 100

⑥ **D** 163

④ **E** 10

④ **E** 100

⑤ **E** 14

⑦ **B** 31

⑥ **D** 127

⑥ **E** 60/20

③ **E** 60

④ **E** 44

⑦ **B** 156

⑦ **B** 156

⑥ **D** 156

③ **D** 31

⑥ **E** 21

④ **E** 8

④ **B** 156

⑥ **D** 100/101

⑦ **B** 133

⑧ **D** 102

⑧ **E** 60

⑤ **E** 14

shown at 70% actual finished size

S T I T C H E S

① Running Stitch *(page 133)*
② Straight Stitch Rose
   (page 115)
③ Japanese Ribbon Stitch
   (page 131)
④ Lazy Daisy Stitch *(page 132)*
⑤ French Knot Stitch
   (page 130)
⑥ Straight Stitch *(page 135)*
⑦ Stem Stitch *(page 134)*
⑧ Satin Stitch *(page 134)*

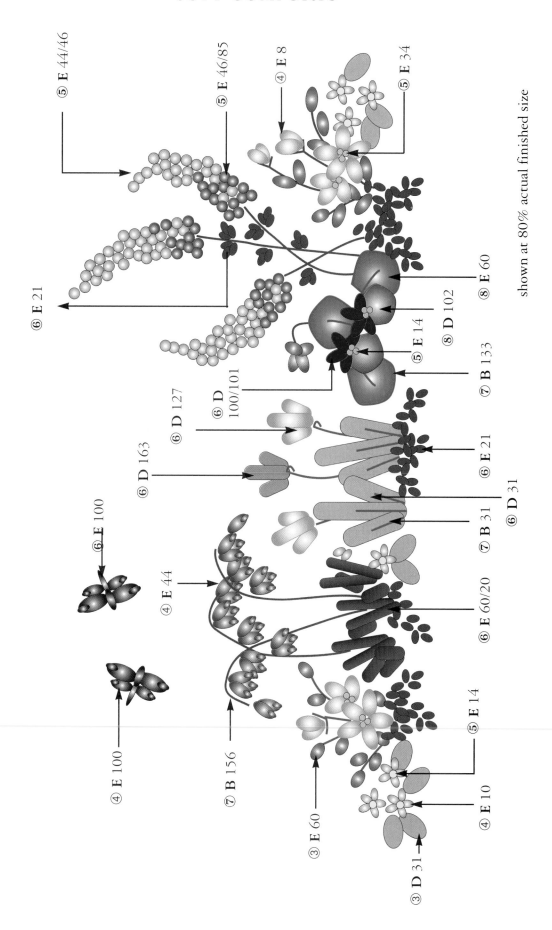

⑤ E 44/46

⑤ E 46/85

④ E 8

⑤ E 34

⑥ E 21

⑧ E 60

⑧ D 102

⑤ E 14

⑧ B 133

⑥ D 127

⑥ D 100/101

⑥ D 163

⑥ E 21

⑥ D 31

⑦ B 31

⑥ E 100

④ E 44

⑥ E 60/20

⑤ E 14

④ E 100

⑦ B 156

③ E 60

④ E 10

③ D 31

shown at 80% actual finished size

JUST *for* BABY

Welcome Keepsakes for the New Arrival

Extending a warm welcome to a new arrival is one of the

great joys of life. Here and on the following pages, you'll

find silk ribbon embroidery embellishment inspirations

for a blessing gown, bonnet, quilt and keepsake sampler

to record the good news for time and eternity.

BLESSING GOWN & BONNET

This lacy, smocked blessing gown was adapted by Esther's namesake daughter, Esther Russell, from the very same tiny pink dress she wore as an infant.

Now that daughter Esther has created a pattern, the original gown is likely destined to be a blessing to many more generations! In the future, the addition of lovingly handstitched silk-ribbon-embroidery embellishments may even make it a double-blessing for the new arrival!

MATERIALS

FABRIC
White blessing gown and matching bonnet

EMBROIDERY THREAD
Kanagawa 380 denier silk embroidery thread (**C**) in each of the following colors: light salmon (94), light blue (120), and light spring green (166)

SILK EMBROIDERY RIBBON
5-yard (4.5m) reel of YLI 7-mm silk embroidery ribbon (**D**) in: peach (39)
5-yard (4.5m) reel of YLI 4-mm silk embroidery ribbon (**E**) in: light blue (125)

ADDITIONAL MATERIALS
Crewel needle - No. 8
Chenille needle - No. 24, No. 26

Following the pattern with the coded reference for stitches, materials, and colors, work the embroidery. For the blessing gown, begin by embellishing the collar and neckline of the bodice and repeat the small scallops of bullion roses around the lower edge of the skirt. For the bonnet, work the floral motif on the smocked brim.

GOWN

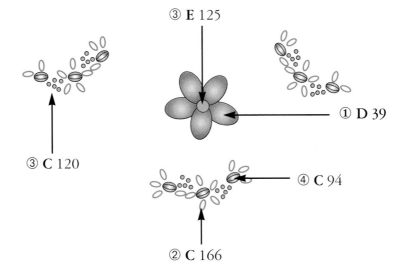

③ E 125

① D 39

③ C 120

④ C 94

② C 166

*The precious rosebuds
on the blessing gown
and matching bonnet
are bullion roses. To
make a rose, work a
single bullion knot
wrapping the needle
five to nine times.
Work two more
bullion knots one
above, and one below
the first, allowing
them to gently
surround the center of
the rose.*

BONNET

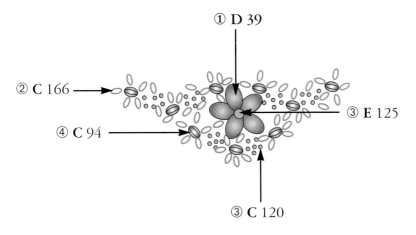

① D 39

② C 166

④ C 94

③ E 125

③ C 120

shown actual finished size

STITCHES

① Japanese Ribbon Stitch
   (page 131)
② Lazy Daisy Stitch *(page 132)*
③ French Knot Stitch *(page 130)*
④ Bullion Rose *(page 138)*

BIRTH ANNOUNCEMENT SAMPLER

Brighten a corner of the nursery and share the good news with an embellished sampler to enjoy now and treasure forever!
Esther Russell created this charming

keepsake for her daughter, Rebecca Ann, using a winning combination of silk ribbon embroidery, shadow embroidery, and several simple embroidery stitches.

MATERIALS

FABRIC
1-9x11-inch (23x28-cm) piece
  of white fabric

EMBROIDERY THREAD
Kanagawa 380 denier silk
  embroidery thread (C) in each
  of the following colors: white,
  light blue (120), and light
  spring green (166)

SILK EMBROIDERY RIBBON
5-yard (4.5m) reel of YLI 2-mm
  silk embroidery ribbon (F) in:
  pink (5)

ADDITIONAL MATERIALS
Silver heart charm
Chenille needle - No. 26
Crewel needle - No. 8

Welcome your new little one by artfully arranging baby's name, birthdate,

weight and size in the spaces between the rows created by the sampler's

embroidered motifs. Use white Kanagawa 380 denier silk embroidery thread to

work each of the script letters and numerals in running stitches.

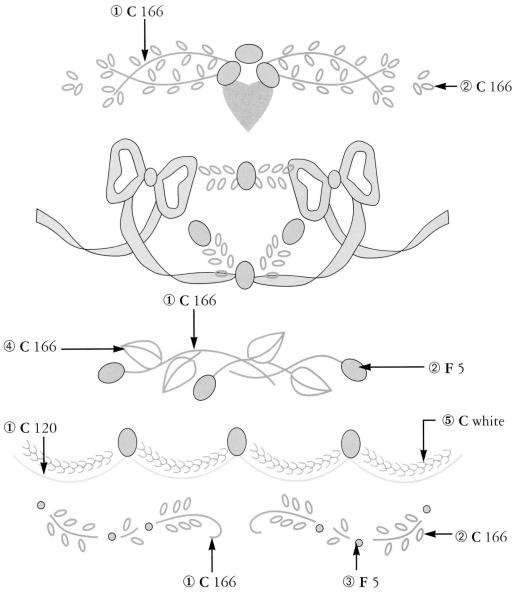

① C 166
② C 166
① C 166
④ C 166
② F 5
① C 120
⑤ C white
① C 166
② C 166
③ F 5

shown actual finished size

STITCHES

① Stem Stitch *(page 134)*
② Lazy Daisy Stitch *(page 132)*
③ French Knot Stitch *(page 130)*
④ Satin Stitch *(page 134)*
⑤ Feather Stitch *(page 128)*

Looking much like intertwined hearts, the bows on the sampler are worked in shadow embroidery. Lightly trace the bows with a water soluble marker.

Work herringbone stitches to fill the shapes from the wrong side of the embroidery. The right side will only show tiny outline running stitches while the wrong side will be completely filled in.

The threads on the wrong side will lightly color the right side leaving just a slight shadow—hence the name, shadow embroidery!

To accent your completed sampler add a delicate silver heart charm nestled on the spray of pink flowers near the top.

BABY'S FIRST QUILT

For baby's first quilt, only the best will do! Esther Randall used silk batiste for the background of this exquisite quilted masterpiece. The lace-bordered center medallion features five floral sprays clustered around an actual silk ribbon bow.

The bow is outlined with feather stitches to hold it in place and additional streamers are added using the same fine silk thread for outlining. The finished piece can be hand- or machine-quilted using a variety of time-honored quilting motifs.

More than twenty years ago, Esther and her husband, Dan, blended their families.

As a result, they are now a pair of proud grandparents 22 times over!

Since only eight of the grandchildren are girls, Esther chose to make her basic quilt design versatile enough that with a simple substitution of colors she and Dan can welcome boys as well as girls into the ever-growing family!

MATERIALS

FABRIC
1–36x48-inch (91.5x123-cm) piece of pastel pink silk batiste

EMBROIDERY THREAD
Kanagawa 1000 denier silk embroidery thread (**B**) in each of the following colors: pink (12), and dark antique mauve (821)
Kanagawa 380 denier silk embroidery thread (**C**) in each of the following colors: light green (31), and light blue (120)

SILK EMBROIDERY RIBBON
5-yard (4.5m) reel of YLI 7-mm silk embroidery ribbon (**D**) in each of the following colors: white (3), light sage green (31), and rose (68)

5-yard (4.5m) reel of YLI 4-mm silk embroidery ribbon (**E**) in each of the following colors: light yellow (14), and light blue (125)
5-yard (4.5m) reel of YLI 13-mm silk embroidery ribbon (**G**) in: light blue (125)

ADDITIONAL MATERIALS
Light blue silk sewing thread
Crewel needle – No. 7
Chenille needle – No. 18, No. 24, and No. 26

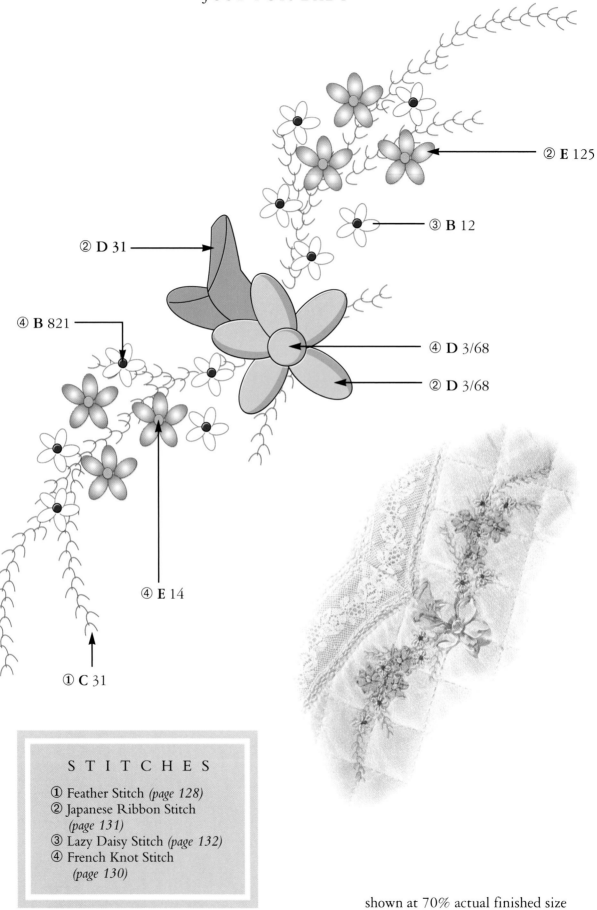

② **E** 125

③ **B** 12

② **D** 31

④ **B** 821

④ **D** 3/68

② **D** 3/68

④ **E** 14

① **C** 31

S T I T C H E S

① Feather Stitch *(page 128)*
② Japanese Ribbon Stitch
 (page 131)
③ Lazy Daisy Stitch *(page 132)*
④ French Knot Stitch
 (page 130)

shown at 70% actual finished size

54

To create this impressive textured dimensional bow for the center of the quilt, enlarge the pattern below 200%.

Tie a length of 13mm ribbon into a bow the same size as the enlarged copy.

Pin the ribbon bow in place on the quilt, folding the ribbon loops as shown so they lay flat. Baste or tack additional streamers in place, as desired.

To secure the bow and streamers, outline all the edges with feather stitches worked in Kanagawa 380 denier silk thread.

shown at 50% actual finished size

FOR HEART
a n d
HOME

Glorious Gifts and Elegant Accents

Grace your home or gift a friend with a splendid

collection of embellished projects ranging from quick-

and-easy to those a bit more challenging.

Start with the finely-crafted laptop desk you can

purchase pre-finished and ready to embellish with an

unusual lining—your silk ribbon embroidery

masterpiece protected with a framed-glass insert.

You'll find more gifts that are pretty as well as

practical on the following pages. All are ready

for your finishing touches and sure to win a special

place in hearts and homes because they're handcrafted

by you with love.

LAPTOP STATIONERY DESK

It's easy to jot off a quick note when everything is handily stored in one convenient place—like this laptop stationery desk that is portable as well!

The purchased desk itself becomes a surprising showcase for silk ribbon embroidery when lined with your finished floral masterpiece (see Sources).

To protect and preserve the stitchery, position a framed sheet of glass inside the box about an inch above the raised silk ribbon floral motifs.

Tulips take center stage on this silk ribbon embroidery. Surprisingly simple, they are easily created by working a combination of two bullion tipped lazy daisy stitches and a Japanese ribbon stitch. Begin each tulip by working a single bullion tipped lazy daisy stitch and then position a second one directly beside it, this time wrapping the stitch from right to left. Complete the tulip with a Japanese ribbon stitch for the center petal.

MATERIALS

FABRIC
14x14-inch (35.5x35.5-cm) piece of lilac 100% wool challis

EMBROIDERY THREAD
YLI 601 fine metallic thread (**A**): Gold (GLD)
Kanagawa 1000 denier silk embroidery thread (**B**) in each of the following colors: light pink (12), spring green (31), green (165), and antique violet (190)
Kanagawa 380 denier silk embroidery thread (**C**) in each of the following colors: green (165), and lilac (187)

SILK EMBROIDERY RIBBON
5-yard (4.5m) reel of YLI 7-mm silk embroidery ribbon (**D**) in: light yellow (156)

5-yard (4.5m) reel of YLI 4-mm silk embroidery ribbon (**E**) in each of the following colors: pink (8), light green (31), teal (64), burgundy (84), periwinkle (118), and medium pink (122)
5-yard (4.5m) reel of YLI 2-mm silk embroidery ribbon (**F**) in each of the following colors: lavender (22), light green (32), and blue (126)

ADDITIONAL MATERIALS
AK Designs lavender seed beads (11/405)
Beading monocord
Tapestry needle - No. 24
Milliner's needle - No. 7
Between needle - No. 10
Beading needle - No.10
Darning needle - No.7

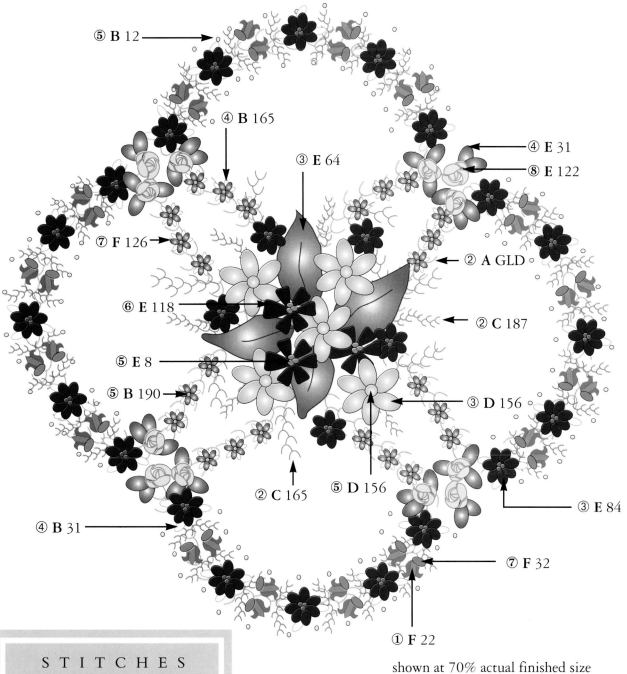

⑤ B 12

④ B 165

③ E 64

④ E 31

⑧ E 122

⑦ F 126

② A GLD

⑥ E 118

② C 187

⑤ E 8

⑤ B 190

③ D 156

② C 165

⑤ D 156

③ E 84

④ B 31

⑦ F 32

① F 22

shown at 70% actual finished size

STITCHES

① Bullion Tipped Lazy Daisy
   Stitch *(page 126)*
② Feather Stitch *(page 128)*
③ Japanese Ribbon Stitch
   (page 131)
④ Lazy Daisy Stitch *(page 132)*
⑤ French Knot Stitch
   (page 130)
⑥ Looped Petal Stitch
   (page 132)
⑦ Straight Stitch *(page 135)*
⑧ Spiral Rose *(page 140)*

CRYSTAL AND CERAMIC JAR LIDS

Ribbon weaving is showcased when the completed lattice is wreathed in florals and framed in the lid of a lovely pastel porcelain jar. Petite purple flowers are perfect for the elegant crystal jar lid, also shown below. Following the pattern with the coded reference for stitches, materials, and colors, work the embroidery.

MATERIALS

FABRIC
6x6-inch (15.2x15.2-cm) pieces of silk broadcloth or wool challis

EMBROIDERY THREAD
Kanagawa 1000 denier silk embroidery thread (**B**) in each of the following colors: light pink (12), light green (31), and old rose (190)
Kanagawa 380 denier silk embroidery thread (**C**) in: spring green (165)

SILK EMBROIDERY RIBBON
5-yard (4.5m) reel of YLI 4-mm silk embroidery ribbon (**E**) in each of the following colors: pink (8), yellow (14), light green (18), light purple (22), medium green (32), blue (44), burgundy (84), light blue (125), and rose (128)
5-yard (4.5m) reel of YLI 2-mm silk embroidery ribbon (**F**) in each of the following colors: pink (8), light green (31), medium green (32), aqua (81), and lavender (101)

ADDITIONAL MATERIALS
AK Designs seed beads: pearl (11/002), light pink (11/306), and lavender (11/405)
Beading monocord
Beading needle – No. 10
Chenille needle – No. 26
Tapestry needle – No. 26
Milliner's needle – No. 7

To create the effect of lattice or a woven basket using silk ribbon, refer to the general instructions *for the woven ribbon stitch on page 137 of the Step-by-Step Guide to the Stitches. This stitch is an* *excellent choice for working a raised, stuffed area such as a padded jar or box lid.*

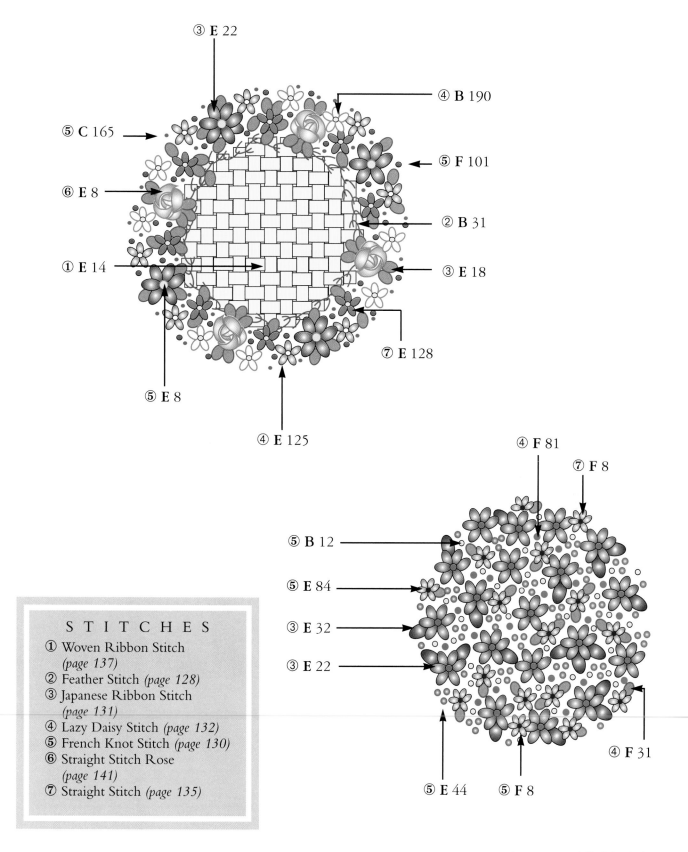

③ **E** 22

④ **B** 190

⑤ **C** 165

⑤ **F** 101

⑥ **E** 8

② **B** 31

① **E** 14

③ **E** 18

⑦ **E** 128

⑤ **E** 8

④ **E** 125

④ **F** 81

⑦ **F** 8

⑤ **B** 12

⑤ **E** 84

③ **E** 32

③ **E** 22

④ **F** 31

⑤ **E** 44

⑤ **F** 8

STITCHES
① Woven Ribbon Stitch
(page 137)
② Feather Stitch *(page 128)*
③ Japanese Ribbon Stitch
(page 131)
④ Lazy Daisy Stitch *(page 132)*
⑤ French Knot Stitch *(page 130)*
⑥ Straight Stitch Rose
(page 141)
⑦ Straight Stitch *(page 135)*

shown actual finished size

FRAMED HEART

The lyrics to a favorite old song say it best, "When I give my heart, it will be forever." And embellishing with silk ribbon embroidery is the perfect way to make a gift that is truly from the heart!

Lightly outline the heart shape on wool challis with a water soluble marker to help in the placement of

the silk ribbon flowers. Once complete, sketch the bow and trailing ribbons. Outline the sections with stem

stitches worked with 1000 denier silk embroidery thread and then fill in with French knots.

MATERIALS

FABRIC
1-16x16-inch (40.6x40.6-cm) piece of ivory wool challis (For a kit, see Sources.)

EMBROIDERY THREAD
Kanagawa 1000 denier silk embroidery thread (**B**) in each of the following colors: light pink (12), spring green (31), blue (33), olive green (156), and eggplant (819)

SILK EMBROIDERY RIBBON
5-yard (4.5m) reel of YLI 7-mm silk embroidery ribbon (**D**) in each of the following colors: pink (7), blue (10), medium green (32), burgundy (84), eggplant (85), raspberry (146), and ivory (156)

5-yard (4.5m) reel of YLI 4-mm silk embroidery ribbon (**E**) in: yellow (14), spring green (18), light green (31), medium green (32), light blue (125), rose (128), and antique violet (178)

5-yard (4.5m) reel of YLI 2-mm silk embroidery ribbon (**F**) in: lavender (23), medium green (32), and coral (122)

ADDITIONAL MATERIALS
Tapestry needle – No. 24
Milliner's needle – No. 7
Between needle – No. 10
Darning needle – No.7

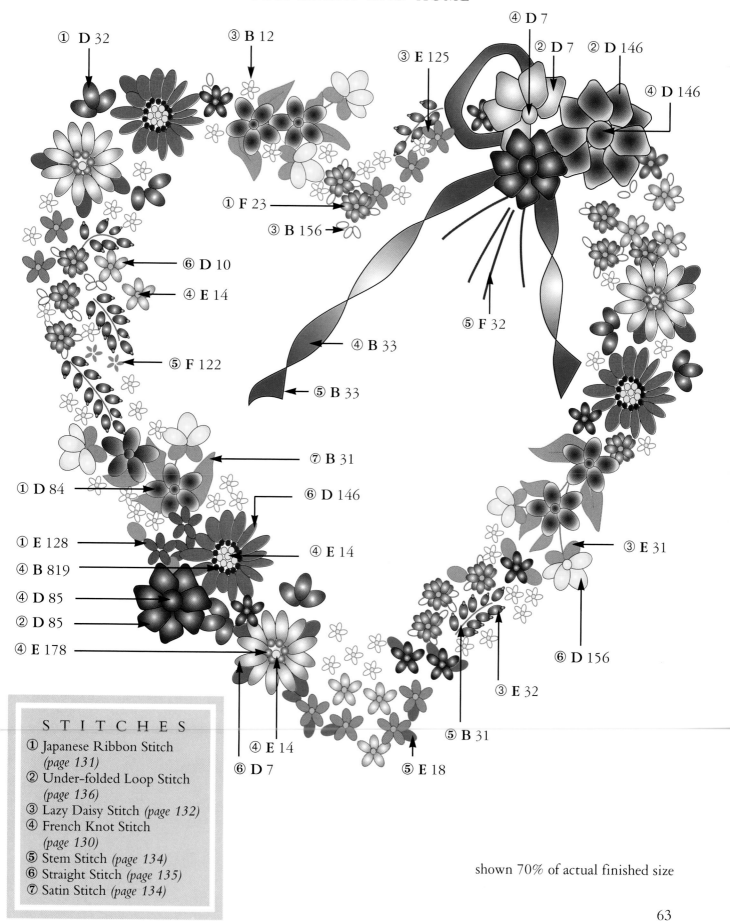

① D 32

③ B 12

④ D 7

② D 7   ② D 146

③ E 125

④ D 146

① F 23

③ B 156

⑥ D 10

④ E 14

⑤ F 32

⑤ F 122

④ B 33

⑤ B 33

⑦ B 31

① D 84

⑥ D 146

① E 128

④ E 14

④ B 819

④ D 85

② D 85

③ E 31

④ E 178

⑥ D 156

④ E 14

③ E 32

⑥ D 7

⑤ B 31

⑤ E 18

STITCHES

① Japanese Ribbon Stitch
   (page 131)
② Under-folded Loop Stitch
   (page 136)
③ Lazy Daisy Stitch *(page 132)*
④ French Knot Stitch
   (page 130)
⑤ Stem Stitch *(page 134)*
⑥ Straight Stitch *(page 135)*
⑦ Satin Stitch *(page 134)*

shown 70% of actual finished size

63

THE SCRIPT LETTER "B"

Personalize a pillow or other decorative accessories for the home with a monogram using a letter selected from your favorite embroidery alphabet.

Lightly trace the main shape of the letter to the center of the fabric. Following the pattern with the coded reference for stitches, materials, and colors, work the embroidery.

This exquisite script letter "B" is worked in Esther Randall's unique style developed over many years of creative stitching. When completed, Esther's flowing script letters take on the appearance of a lavish floral bouquet fresh-picked from the garden.

MATERIALS

FABRIC
10x10-inch (25.4x25.4-cm) piece
    of silk broadcloth or wool challis

EMBROIDERY THREAD
YLI 601 fine metallic thread (**A**):
    Gold (GLD)
Kanagawa 1000 denier silk
    embroidery thread (**B**) in each of
    the following colors: light pink
    (12), and light green (31)
Kanagawa 380 denier silk
    embroidery thread (**C**) in:
    light green (31)

SILK EMBROIDERY RIBBON
5-yard (4.5m) reel of YLI 7-mm
    silk embroidery ribbon (**D**) in
    each of the following colors:
    lavender (23), medium green (32),
    and rose (128)

5-yard (4.5m) reel of YLI 4-mm
    silk embroidery ribbon (**E**) in:
    rose (128)
5-yard (4.5m) reel of YLI 2-mm silk
    embroidery ribbon (**F**) in each of
    the following colors: yellow (14),
    light lavender (22), dark purple
    (85), eggplant (86), light rose (111),
    light blue (115), and
    bright rose (128)

ADDITIONAL MATERIALS
AK Designs seed beads: light pink
    (11/308)
Beading monocord
Beading needle - No. 10
Chenille needle - No. 26
Crewel needle -   No. 7

STITCHES
① Japanese Ribbon Stitch
   (page 131)
② Couching Stitch
   (page 127)
③ Lazy Daisy Stitch
   (page 132)
④ French Knot Stitch
   (page 130)
⑤ Feather Stitch *(page 128)*

① F 115 → ① F 85/86 ⑤ C 31

① D 128 →

① E 128 →

③ B 12 →

④ E 128

① F 22 → ① D 32

② F 111

③ B 31 ④ F 14 ⑤ A GLD

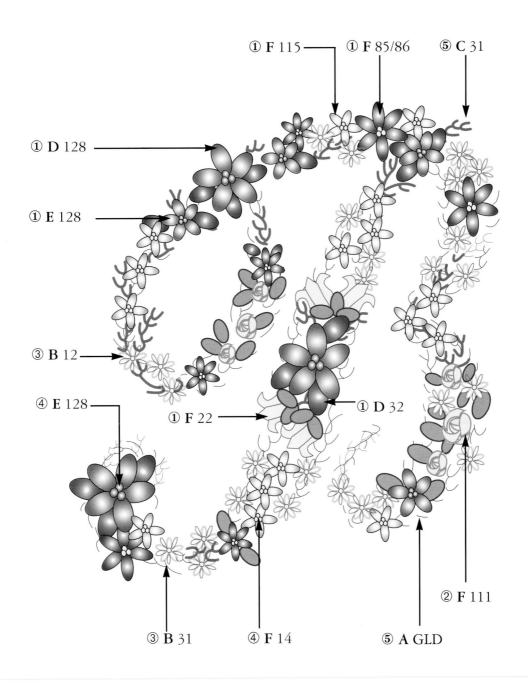

shown actual finished size

GLOVE AND SCARF BOX

An impressive accent for the front hall table, this handsome lidded box serves a practical purpose as well, since scarves and gloves will always be close at hand (see Sources). Because the top and side-panel inserts accommodating the finished stitchery are inside-mounted, the box maintains the appearance of a finely crafted heirloom. Following the pattern with the coded reference for stitches, materials, and colors, work the embroidery.

Silk ribbon is so versatile that you can stitch on almost any texture of fabric— even silk itself!

Esther chose to personalize her glove and scarf box by using the rich green silk from the dress she wore to

the weddings of two of her four children. For Esther, the box is now a joyful reminder of cherished memories.

MATERIALS

FABRIC
1-11x15-inch (27.9x38.1-cm), 2-11x7-inch (27.9x17.8-cm), and 2-7x15-inch (17.8x38.1-cm) pieces of green silk

EMBROIDERY THREAD
Kanagawa 1000 denier silk embroidery thread (**B**) in each of the following colors: blue (33), green (156), and spring green (165)

SILK EMBROIDERY RIBBON
5-yard (4.5m) reel of YLI 7-mm silk embroidery ribbon (**D**) in each of the following colors: pink (8), yellow (14), light green (31), medium green (32), green (33), eggplant (85), and ivory (156)
5-yard (4.5m) reel of YLI 4-mm silk embroidery ribbon (**E**) in each of the following colors: pink (8), light yellow (12), yellow (14), medium green (32), peach (39), burgundy (84), light lavender (100), light purple (102), sky blue (124), light blue (125), and rose (129)
5-yard (4.5m) reel of YLI 2-mm silk embroidery ribbon (**F**) in: medium green (32)

ADDITIONAL MATERIALS
Chenille needle - No. 24, No. 26
Crewel needle -   No. 7
Milliner's needle - No. 7

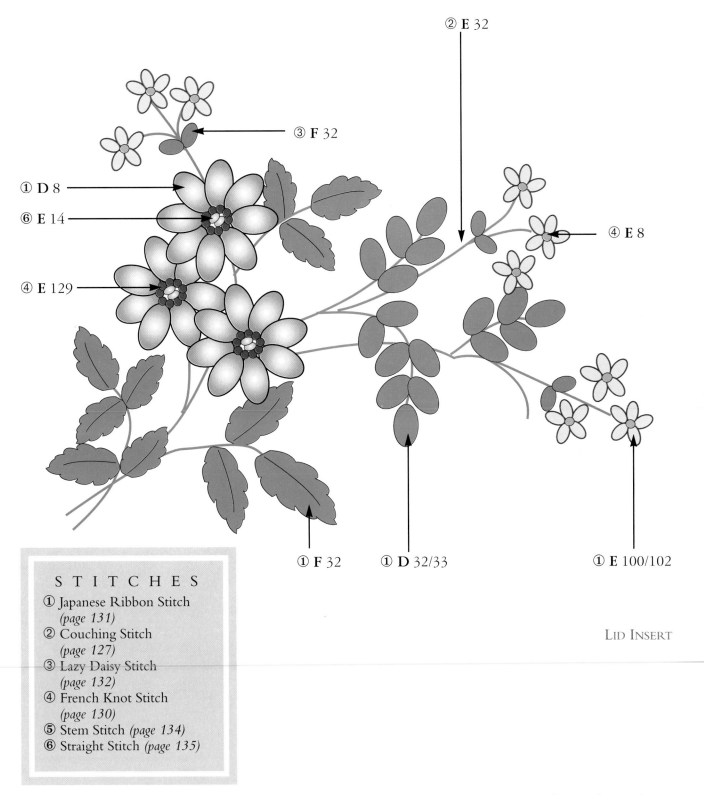

② **E** 32

③ **F** 32

① **D** 8

⑥ **E** 14

④ **E** 129

④ **E** 8

① **F** 32

① **D** 32/33

① **E** 100/102

LID INSERT

STITCHES
① Japanese Ribbon Stitch
   (page 131)
② Couching Stitch
   (page 127)
③ Lazy Daisy Stitch
   (page 132)
④ French Knot Stitch
   (page 130)
⑤ Stem Stitch *(page 134)*
⑥ Straight Stitch *(page 135)*

shown 90% of actual finished size

SIDE PANEL INSERT

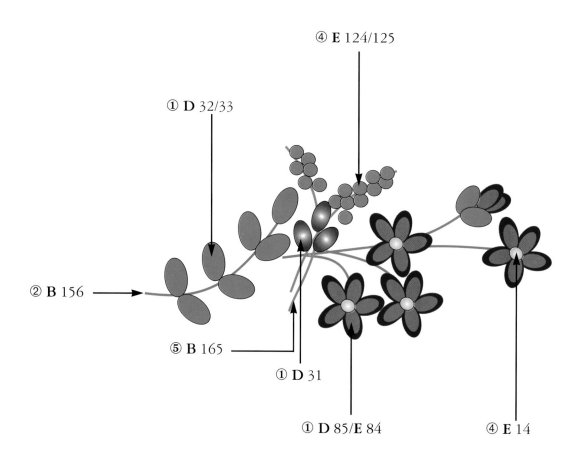

④ **E** 124/125

① **D** 32/33

② **B** 156

⑤ **B** 165

① **D** 31

① **D** 85/**E** 84

④ **E** 14

S T I T C H E S
① Japanese Ribbon Stitch
   (page 131)
② Couching Stitch
   (page 127)
③ Lazy Daisy Stitch
   (page 132)
④ French Knot Stitch
   (page 130)
⑤ Stem Stitch *(page 134)*
⑥ Straight Stitch *(page 135)*

shown 90% of actual finished size

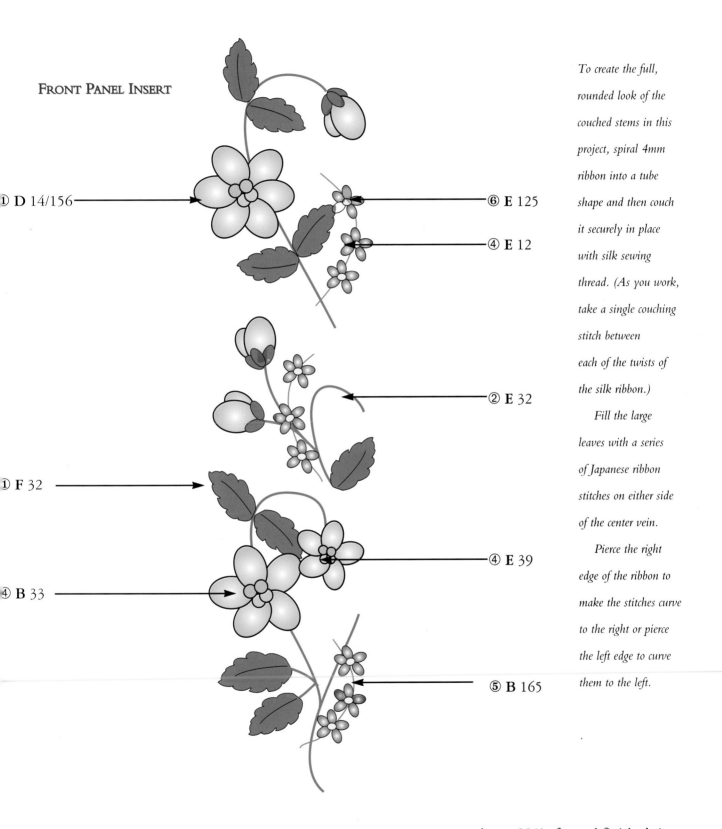

FRONT PANEL INSERT

① D 14/156

⑥ E 125

④ E 12

② E 32

① F 32

④ E 39

④ B 33

⑤ B 165

To create the full, rounded look of the couched stems in this project, spiral 4mm ribbon into a tube shape and then couch it securely in place with silk sewing thread. (As you work, take a single couching stitch between each of the twists of the silk ribbon.)

Fill the large leaves with a series of Japanese ribbon stitches on either side of the center vein.

Pierce the right edge of the ribbon to make the stitches curve to the right or pierce the left edge to curve them to the left.

shown 90% of actual finished size

TREASURE BOX COTTAGE

Finding imaginative ways to use every precious scrap of silk ribbon is a constant challenge for serious needleworkers. Rise to the occasion by covering the walls of a charming cottage box with a miniature silk ribbon embroidery flower garden!

Designed by Norma Restall, the treasure box cottage combines her enthusiasm for embroidery and gardening inspired by all the shapes and colors within her own garden in Wales.

To spark your imagination, the box shown here is actually two gifts in one—a delightful housewarming keepsake and a wonderful treasure box as well. The lid is constructed so that it lifts off to provide decorative, but useful storage.

For a personalized housewarming gift, try your hand at creating the exterior features of the new homeowner's pride and joy. Make your completed stitchery even more special by embroidering the house numbers or the family name above the front door.

The treasure box featured here is inspired by the designer's love of her native countryside. Imagine how many quaint cottages are nestled at the end of winding country lanes just waiting to be discovered by needle artisans with sketch pads and a palette of silk ribbons for embroidering!

If you'd like to try your hand at replicating this treasure box cottage, the designer's detailed instructions for embroidering, embellishing, and then constructing the cottage are available in a six-page booklet (see Sources).

SMALL
ENDEARMENTS

Accessories With the Personal Touch

Ribbons, roses, buttons, and lace—these are the fine makings

for personalized accessories and romantic keepsakes that will

be remembered with love for years to come.

To recreate the aura of the gilded age, choose from a

dazzling array of petite treasures and traditional Victorian

needlework accents.

Featured here are just a few of the sewing accessories from

the collection of projects you'll find on the following pages—

an eyeglass case, a needlecase, scissors and spool keepers, a

wrist pincushion and a lace-trimmed pillow for needles and

pins —all lavishly embellished with silk ribbon embroidery

and other delicate trims.

NEEDLES & PINS PILLOW

Because the Victorians had a passion for flowers, many of the parlors and sun-drenched porches in turn-of-the century homes were filled with vases bursting with blooms and accented by leafy green potted plants like the Boston fern.

Reminiscent of that era, contributing designer Merry Nader, has successfully blended florals with ferns in the pleasing combination on the pillow shown below.

MATERIALS

FABRIC
1-10x15-inch (25.5x38-cm)
    piece of ivory wool gabardine
Purchased ribbon-roses "by the
    yard" trim (See Sources.)

EMBROIDERY THREAD
Kanagawa 1000 denier silk
    embroidery thread (**B**) in each
    of the following colors: olive
    green (156), gray green (157),
    and tan (814)

SILK EMBROIDERY RIBBON
5-yard (4.5m) reel of YLI 7-mm
    silk embroidery ribbon (**D**) in
    each of the following colors:
    pink (7), yellow (14), green
    (20), peach (39), dark red (49),
    and mauve (163)
5-yard (4.5m) reel of YLI 4-mm
    silk embroidery ribbon (**E**) in
    each of the following colors:
    antique violet (178), and dark
    antique violet (179)

ADDITIONAL MATERIALS
Chenille needle - No. 24, No. 26
Milliner's needle - No. 7

To achieve additional depth and shading when creating the pink web stitch rose, use two shades of the same color of silk ribbon. Work the center of each rose in the darker shade and then use the lighter shade for adding the outside petals.

③ **D** 49

⑥ **D** 14

① **D** 39   ⑤ **D** 20

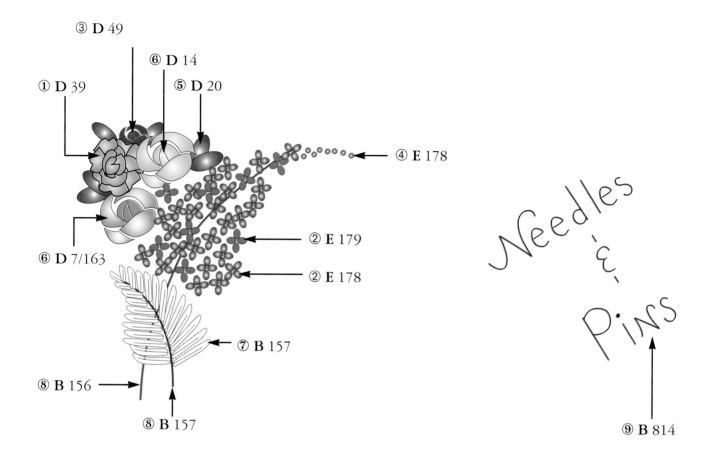

④ **E** 178

② **E** 179

⑥ **D** 7/163

② **E** 178

Needles & Pins

⑦ **B** 157

⑧ **B** 156

⑧ **B** 157

⑨ **B** 814

STITCHES
① Rouched Rose *(page 140)*
② Straight Stitch *(page 135)*
③ Straight Stitch Rose
   (page 141)
④ French Knot Stitch
   (page 130)
⑤ Japanese Ribbon Stitch
   (page 131)
⑥ Web Stitch Rose
   (page 141)
⑦ Satin Stitch *(page 134)*
⑧ Stem Stitch *(page 134)*
⑨ Running Stitch *(page 133)*

shown 70% actual finished size

SCISSORS & SPOOL KEEPERS

Keeping scissors, ribbon spools or floss skeins close at hand is easy when you stow them in embellished satin cases that can be suspended on slender satin cording. Lavish each little case with clusters of ribbon flowers and wear it as you would an elegant pendant necklace—truly a fashion statement for the dedicated stitcher!

Merry Nader's collection of Victorian-inspired sewing accessories is an excellent example of how ornately-embellished projects like these can also serve a practical purpose.

Taking a close look at the background fern on the scissors case, note how Merry has given the tendrils a realistic look by stitching with embroidery wool.

MATERIALS

FABRIC
1-6x10-inch (15x25-cm) piece of ivory wool challis for scissor case front and flap
1-6x7-inch (15x18-cm) piece of ivory wool challis for spool bag

EMBROIDERY THREAD
Royal Stitch Embroidery Wool (**A**) in: green (60)
Kanagawa 1000 denier silk embroidery thread (**B**) in each of the following colors: dark green (132), brown-green (157), and moss (160)

SILK EMBROIDERY RIBBON
5-yard (4.5m) reel of YLI 7-mm silk embroidery ribbon (**D**) in each of the following colors: pink (8), yellow (13), salmon (24), peach (29), khaki green (56), and mauve (163)
5-yard (4.5m) reel of YLI 4-mm silk embroidery ribbon (**E**) in each of the following colors: dark green 21), blue (44), red (49), gold (54), antique rose (112), periwinkle (118), yellow green (170), apricot (172), and magenta (181)
5-yard (4.5m) reel of YLI 2-mm silk embroidery ribbon (**F**) in: green (33)

ADDITIONAL MATERIALS
Chenille needle - No. 24, No. 26
Milliner's needle - No. 7

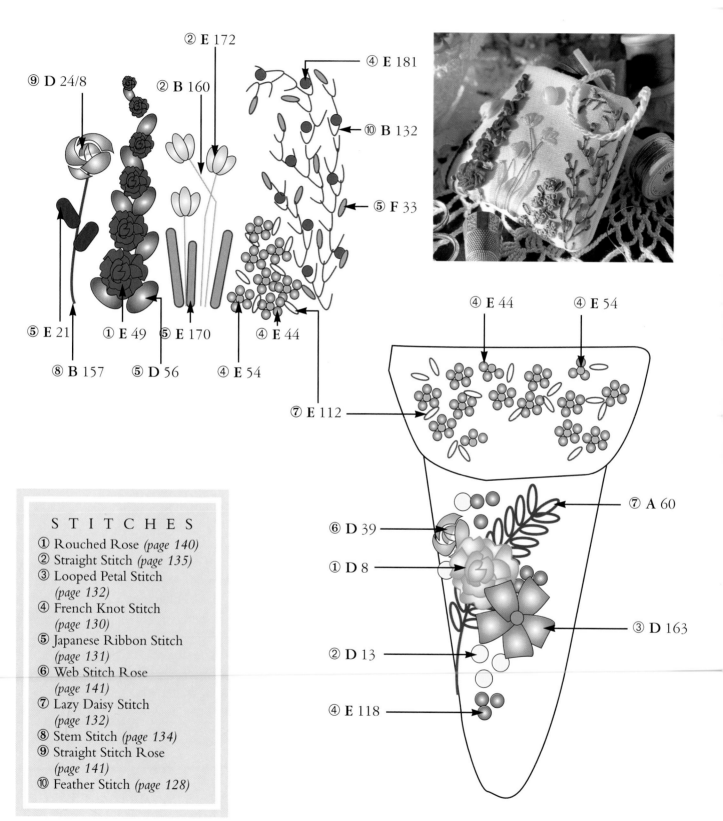

② E 172

⑨ D 24/8

② B 160

④ E 181

⑩ B 132

⑤ F 33

⑤ E 21

① E 49

⑤ E 170

④ E 44

⑧ B 157

⑤ D 56

④ E 54

④ E 44

④ E 54

⑦ E 112

⑦ A 60

⑥ D 39

① D 8

③ D 163

② D 13

④ E 118

STITCHES
① Rouched Rose *(page 140)*
② Straight Stitch *(page 135)*
③ Looped Petal Stitch
(page 132)
④ French Knot Stitch
(page 130)
⑤ Japanese Ribbon Stitch
(page 131)
⑥ Web Stitch Rose
(page 141)
⑦ Lazy Daisy Stitch
(page 132)
⑧ Stem Stitch *(page 134)*
⑨ Straight Stitch Rose
(page 141)
⑩ Feather Stitch *(page 128)*

shown actual finished size

79

NEEDLECASE & WRIST CUSHION

A needlecase and wrist cushion for needles and pins are essential sewing accessories for the serious stitcher.

The striking pair shown on these pages will make a handsome addition to any workbasket.

Both the web stitch rose (featured on the needlecase), and the pink straight stitch rose (featured on the wrist pincushion) take center stage when worked on black wool.

The straight stitch rose is given extra dimension by working the center of the flower in the darker color and the outer petals in the lighter color.

MATERIALS

FABRIC
1-10x6-inch (25.5x15-cm) piece of black wool felt for needlecase, and
1-6x6-inch (15x15-cm) piece of black wool felt for wrist pincushion

SILK EMBROIDERY RIBBON
5-yard (4.5m) reel of YLI 7-mm silk embroidery ribbon (**D**) in each of the following colors: pink (8), beige (51), magenta (146), light yellow (156), and peach (172)
5-yard (4.5m) reel of YLI 4-mm silk embroidery ribbon (**E**) in each of the following colors: green (20), dark gold (52), bright gold (54), periwinkle (117), pink (122), rose (128), avocado green (171), and antique violet (179)
5-yard (4.5m) reel of YLI 2-mm silk embroidery ribbon (**F**) in: light blue (124)

ADDITIONAL MATERIALS
Chenille needle - No. 24, No. 26

NEEDLECASE

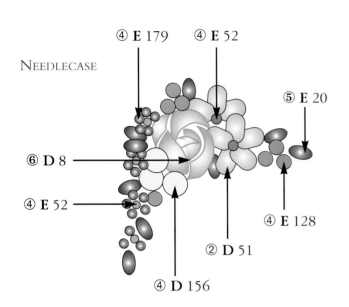

④ E 179   ④ E 52   ⑤ E 20

⑥ D 8

④ E 52

④ D 156   ② D 51   ④ E 128

STITCHES

① Straight Stitch Rose
   (page 141)
② Straight Stitch *(page 135)*
③ Looped Petal Stitch
   (page 132)
④ French Knot Stitch
   (page 130)
⑤ Japanese Ribbon Stitch
   (page 131)
⑥ Web Stitch Rose
   (page 141)
⑦ Lazy Daisy Stitch
   (page 132)

WRIST CUSHION

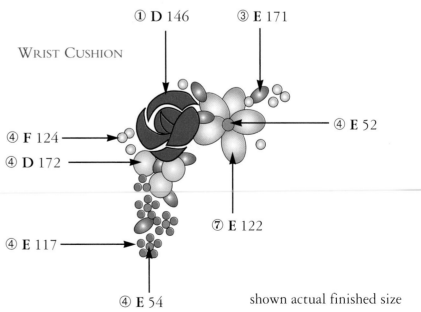

① D 146   ③ E 171

④ F 124   ④ E 52

④ D 172

④ E 117   ⑦ E 122

④ E 54   shown actual finished size

81

EYEGLASS CASE

These delightful floral accents should inspire anyone with an eye for detail to personalize an eyeglass case with silk ribbon embroidery embellishments. Stitch one up from scraps of satin, other soft fabric, or simply enhance the plain purchased variety.

Following the pattern with the coded reference for stitches, materials, and colors work the embroidery. Add your name or initials and make it truly one-of-a kind!

Designer and teacher, Merry Nader, enjoys the challenge of creating dimensional effects for her favorite garden flowers like the iris and sunflower.

The iris is quite easy to capture in silk ribbon embroidery—simply work a lazy daisy stitch and then add three tiny straight stitches at the base of the bloom to form the remaining petals.

MATERIALS

FABRIC
1- 8x11-inch (20x28-cm) piece of ivory wool challis

EMBROIDERY THREAD
Kanagawa 1000 denier silk embroidery thread (**B**) in each of the following colors: dark olive green (26), dark brown (57), green (112), aqua (115), khaki green (157), and yellow green (161)

SILK EMBROIDERY RIBBON
5-yard (4.5m) reel of YLI 7-mm silk embroidery ribbon (**D**) in: olive green (171)
5-yard (4.5m) reel of YLI 4-mm silk embroidery ribbon (**E**) in each of the following colors: dark gold (53), bright gold (54), blue (115), fuchsia (145), mauve (163), olive green (171), peach (172), purple (177), and antique violet (179)

ADDITIONAL MATERIALS
Tapestry needle – No. 24, No. 26

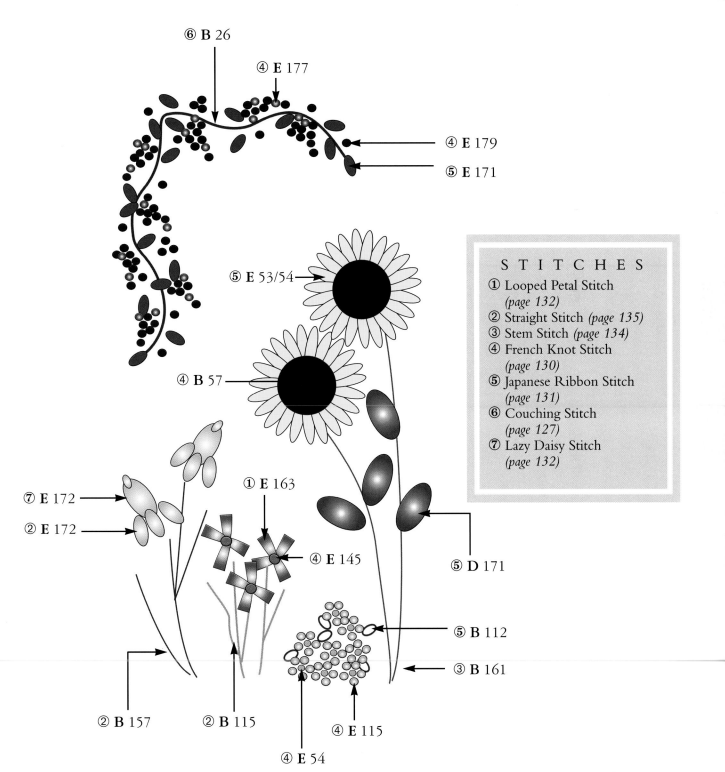

⑥ **B** 26

④ **E** 177

④ **E** 179

⑤ **E** 171

⑤ **E** 53/54

④ **B** 57

⑦ **E** 172

② **E** 172

① **E** 163

④ **E** 145

⑤ **D** 171

⑤ **B** 112

③ **B** 161

② **B** 157

② **B** 115

④ **E** 115

④ **E** 54

S T I T C H E S
① Looped Petal Stitch
   (page 132)
② Straight Stitch *(page 135)*
③ Stem Stitch *(page 134)*
④ French Knot Stitch
   (page 130)
⑤ Japanese Ribbon Stitch
   (page 131)
⑥ Couching Stitch
   (page 127)
⑦ Lazy Daisy Stitch
   (page 132)

shown actual finished size

THE WEDDING CAKE BOX

*The feather stitch is
ideal for laying a
foundation upon
which to put other
silk ribbon flowers.*

*After tracing your
initial onto the fabric,
outline the shape of
the letter with feather
stitches. Following
the pattern with the
coded reference for
stitches, materials,
and colors, work the
embroidery.*

*Note how the
feather stitches add
wisps of back-
ground color and
texture to the
completed stitchery.*

*In the tradition of "To have and to hold
from this day forward…" the wedding cake
box will hold a variety of keepsakes from
the bride's special day—perhaps something
old, something new, something borrowed
and something blue!*

*Begin with a purchased oval lidded box
and cover it with elegant fabric. When the
completed silk ribbon embroidery monogram
is added to the lid of the box, a layer of*

*batting underneath provides a soft, rounded
effect. Top it off with a frosting of lacy
beaded swirls, and the wedding cake box
looks almost good enough to eat!*

*Make the box ahead of time for a bridal-
shower centerpiece, then showcase it again at
the wedding reception as a useful container
for collecting cards and keepsakes at the
table with the guest book.*

MATERIALS

FABRIC
13x15-inch (33x38-cm) pieces
    of silk broadcloth or wool challis

EMBROIDERY THREAD
YLI 601 fine metallic thread (**A**):
    Gold (GLD)
Kanagawa 1000 denier silk
    embroidery thread (**B**) in:
    light green (31)

SILK EMBROIDERY RIBBON
5-yard (4.5m) reel of YLI 7-mm
    silk embroidery ribbon (**D**) in
    each of the following colors:
    yellow (13), and peach (39)

5-yard (4.5m) reel of YLI 4-mm
    silk embroidery ribbon (**E**) in each
    of the following colors: lightest
    pink (5), light pink (8), yellow
    (14), medium green (20), lavender
    (23), green (33), light peach (39),
    peach (42), pink (68), eggplant
    (84), aqua (116), light blue (124),
    blue (125), and mauve (163)

ADDITIONAL MATERIALS
Chenille needle - No. 26
Crewel needle -   No. 7

STITCHES

① Japanese Ribbon Stitch
   (page 131)
② Bullion Tipped Lazy Daisy
   (page 126)
③ Lazy Daisy Stitch
   (page 132)
④ French Knot Stitch
   (page 130)
⑤ Feather Stitch *(page 128)*
⑥ Straight Stitch *(page 135)*

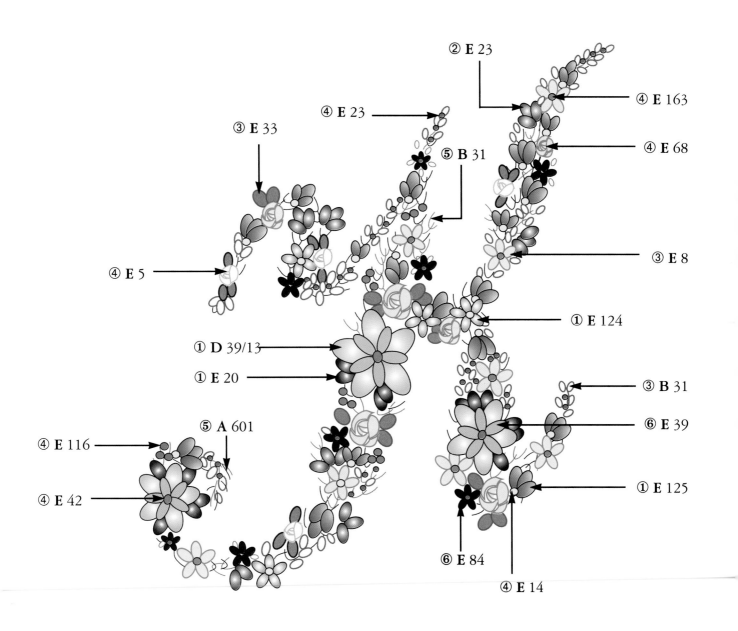

② E 23
④ E 163
④ E 23
④ E 68
③ E 33
⑤ B 31
③ E 8
④ E 5
① E 124
① D 39/13
③ B 31
① E 20
⑥ E 39
⑤ A 601
④ E 116
① E 125
④ E 42
⑥ E 84
④ E 14

shown actual finished size

PILLBOX, PINS & BUTTON COVER

Decorative accents to wear and share include a dahlia button cover, pins, and a hinged-brass pillbox—all embellished with delicate floral details.

The under-folded loop stitch blossoms quickly into a lovely pink dahlia when worked on a covered button form.

Tiny treasures like the pins and the pillbox are also quick-to-make using prefinished brass frames and decorative pin backs (see Sources).

MATERIALS

FABRIC
Scraps of silk broadcloth
  or wool challis

EMBROIDERY THREAD
Kanagawa 1000 denier silk
  embroidery thread (**B**) in each
  of the following colors: light
  pink (12), and salmon (93)

SILK EMBROIDERY RIBBON
5-yard (4.5m) reel of YLI 7-mm
  silk embroidery ribbon (**D**) in
  each of the following colors:
  pink (8), and yellow (14)
5-yard (4.5m) reel of YLI 4-mm
  silk embroidery ribbon (**E**) in
  each of the following colors:
  white (3), blue (10), yellow (14),
  spring green (18), green (31),
  pink (68), bright pink (69),
  aqua (116), rose (128), and
  light yellow (156)
5-yard (4.5m) reel of YLI 2-mm
  silk embroidery ribbon (**F**) in
  each of the following colors:
  avocado green (20), green (31),
  and medium green (32)

ADDITIONAL MATERIALS
Covered button forms
Decorative pin backs
Chenille needle - No. 26
Crewel needle -   No. 7

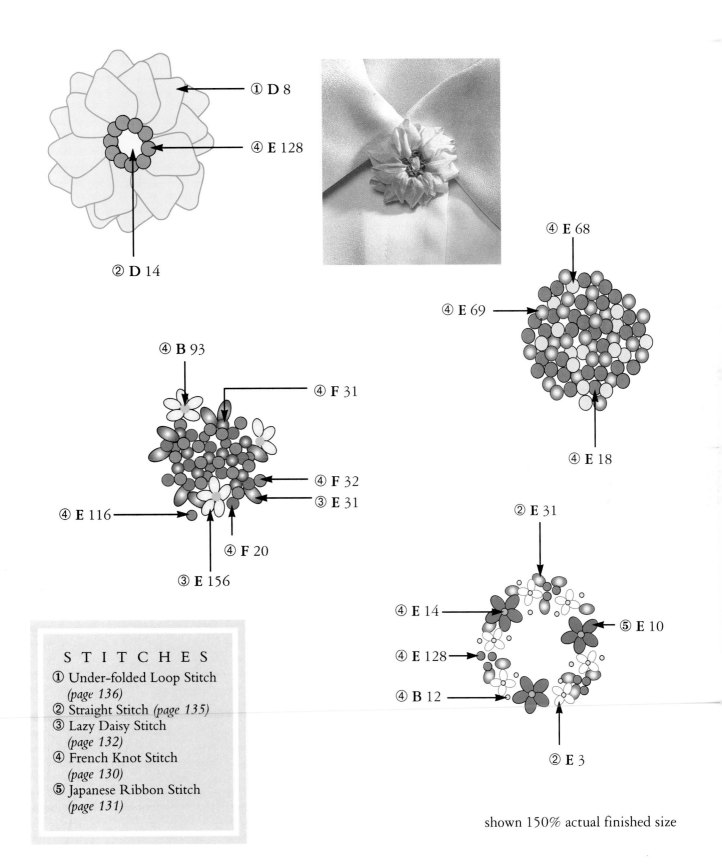

① D 8

④ E 128

② D 14

④ E 68

④ E 69

④ E 18

④ B 93

④ F 31

④ F 32

③ E 31

④ E 116

④ F 20

③ E 156

② E 31

④ E 14

⑤ E 10

④ E 128

④ B 12

② E 3

STITCHES
① Under-folded Loop Stitch
  (page 136)
② Straight Stitch *(page 135)*
③ Lazy Daisy Stitch
  (page 132)
④ French Knot Stitch
  (page 130)
⑤ Japanese Ribbon Stitch
  (page 131)

shown 150% actual finished size

HANDKERCHIEF CASE

For a proper Victorian lady, the necessities for her dressing table almost always included a mirror, comb and brush, and even an embellished case for handkerchiefs. Inspired by the past, this modern-day case will hold everything from jewelry to lingerie. For more nostalgia, personalize other accessories with your own imaginative floral-bordered monogram in a style similar to the ones added to the brush and mirror shown here. (Pattern and instructions for both are featured in Tips and Techniques for Getting Started beginning on page 8.)

To create the glorious tulips on this lace-edged handkerchief case, Esther worked a pair of bullion tipped lazy daisy stitches that face in opposite directions.

To complete the flower, she used a Japanese ribbon stitch as the center petal.

MATERIALS

FABRIC
1-14x24-inch (35.5x61-cm) piece of ivory wool challis

EMBROIDERY THREAD
Kanagawa 1000 denier silk embroidery thread (**B**) in: spring green (165)

SILK EMBROIDERY RIBBON
5-yard (4.5m) reel of YLI 7-mm silk embroidery ribbon (**D**) in each of the following colors: green (33), light yellow (156), and eggplant (177)
5-yard (4.5m) reel of YLI 4-mm silk embroidery ribbon (**E**) in each of the following colors: pink (7), green (32), light aqua (115), light blue (124), and antique rose (163)
5-yard (4.5m) reel of YLI 2-mm silk embroidery ribbon (**F**) in: pink (7), and eggplant (177)

ADDITIONAL MATERIALS
Chenille needle - No. 24, No. 26
Tapestry needle - No. 24

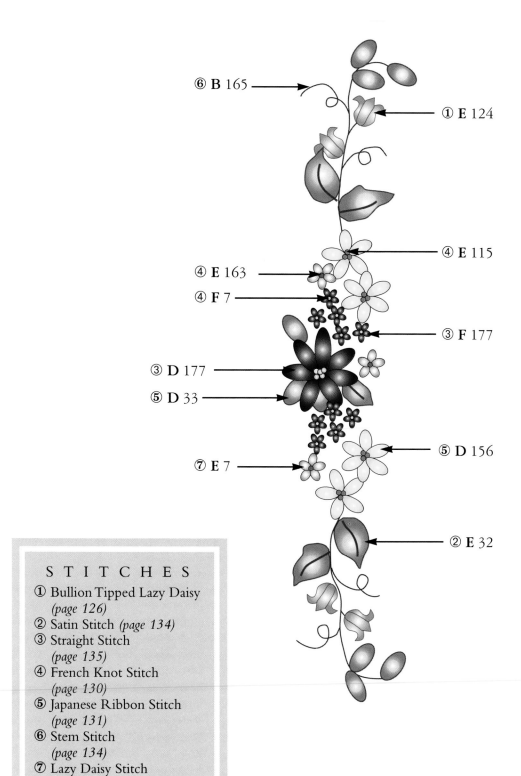

⑥ B 165

① E 124

④ E 115

④ E 163

④ F 7

③ F 177

③ D 177

⑤ D 33

⑤ D 156

⑦ E 7

② E 32

STITCHES
① Bullion Tipped Lazy Daisy
  (page 126)
② Satin Stitch *(page 134)*
③ Straight Stitch
  (page 135)
④ French Knot Stitch
  (page 130)
⑤ Japanese Ribbon Stitch
  (page 131)
⑥ Stem Stitch
  (page 134)
⑦ Lazy Daisy Stitch
  (page 132)

shown 80% actual finished size

PICKET FENCE PURSE

Many of Merry Nader's design inspirations come directly from her impressive collection of antique Victorian crazy quilts. This "picket-fence purse" goes beyond patchwork to incorporate a variety of whimsical embellishments including a silk-ribbon embroidered dragonfly, fence and birdhouse; an appliquéd folk-style fabric sun and moon; a row of rouched ribbon roses; and dozens of loops of hand-beaded fringe.

In her classes, Merry encourages each student to experiment with silk ribbon embroidery and just plain have fun.

Merry suggests folding completed stitches and tacking them into position to create new shapes for leaves and petals.

For example, the flowers at the top of her purse are Japanese ribbon stitches that were worked loosely and then folded to the side and tacked in place to create a gracefully flowing leaf.

MATERIALS

FABRIC
Assorted fabrics – velvets, satins,
and taffeta

EMBROIDERY THREAD
YLI 601 fine metallic thread (**A**):
gold (GLD)
variegated blue/pink (60)
Kanagawa 1000 denier silk
embroidery thread (**B**) in each of
the following colors: black (black),
pink (12), rust (55), periwinkle
(117), light yellow (142), gray
green (157), rose (170),
bright pink (795)
Kanagawa 380 denier silk embroidery
thread (**C**) in each of the following
colors: white (white),
eggplant (22), peach (94),
blue (105), light olive green
(114), gray (129), yellow (142),
olive green (161), melon (175),
salmon (177), light blue (721),
and chartreuse (764)
Royal Stitch Embroidery Wool (**H**)
in: green (60)
Candlelight metallic yarn (**I**) in:
gold/silver (G/S)

SILK EMBROIDERY RIBBON
5-yard (4.5m) reel of YLI 7-mm
silk embroidery ribbon (**D**) in
each of the following colors:
black (4), pink (6), khaki green
(56), light gray (58), peach (167),
and magenta (181)

5-yard (4.5m) reel of YLI 4-mm
silk embroidery ribbon (**E**) in
each of the following colors:
pink (6), green (20), orange (43),
tan (65), eggplant (85), royal
purple (99), salmon (104), apricot
(106), dark rose (129), pink (144),
dark gold (148), dark red (176),
purple (177), and raspberry (181)
5-yard (4.5m) reel of YLI 2-mm
silk embroidery ribbon (**F**) in
each of the following colors:
white (3), pink (6), gold (52), dark
gray (59), light aqua (131), teal
(134), and light yellow (156)
5-yard (4.5m) reel of YLI 13-mm
silk embroidery ribbon (**G**) in
each of the following colors:
white (3), pink (6), and
light yellow (156)

YLI 5-mm spark organdy
embroidery ribbon (**J**) in:
white (W)

ADDITIONAL MATERIALS
Assorted small buttons and sequins
Beading monocord
Beading needle – No. 10
Chenille needle – No. 24, No. 26
Crewel needle – No. 7
Milliner's needle – No. 7

Textile markers and paints can also be used to add details to completed silk ribbon embroidery. The bumble bee at the top left corner of the bead-fringed bag takes on a lifelike appearance with the addition of stripes applied after the embroidery is complete with a black textile marker.

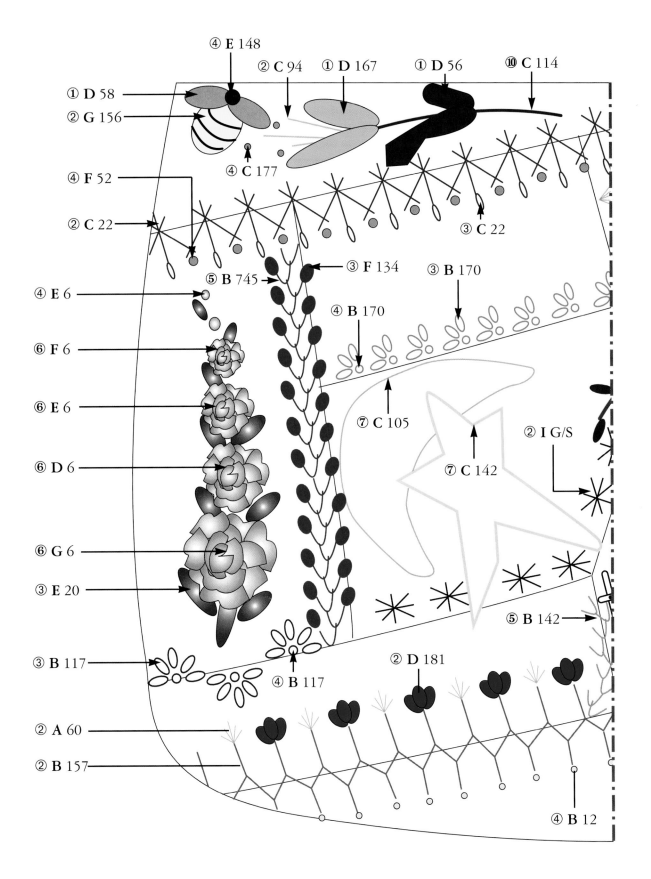

④ E 148
② C 94
① D 167
① D 56
⑩ C 114
① D 58
② G 156
④ C 177
④ F 52
② C 22
③ C 22
③ F 134
③ B 170
⑤ B 745
④ B 170
④ E 6
⑥ F 6
⑦ C 105
⑥ E 6
② I G/S
⑥ D 6
⑦ C 142
⑥ G 6
③ E 20
⑤ B 142
③ B 117
④ B 117
② D 181
② A 60
② B 157
④ B 12

shown 110% actual finished size

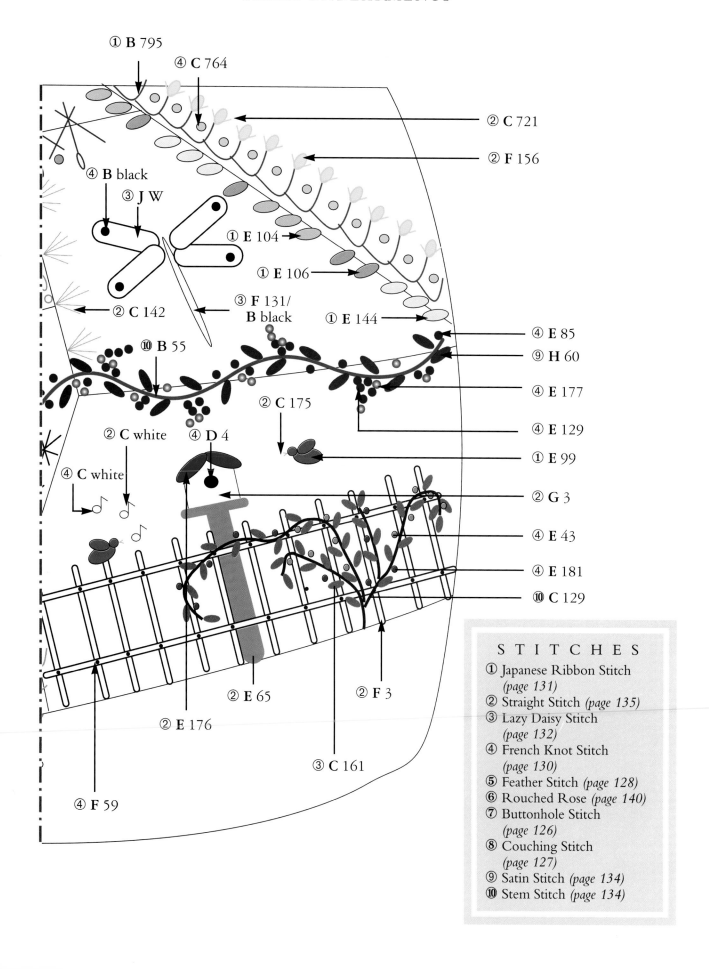

① B 795
④ C 764
② C 721
② F 156
④ B black
③ J W
① E 104
① E 106
② C 142
③ F 131/
B black
① E 144
④ E 85
⑨ H 60
⑩ B 55
④ E 177
② C 175
④ E 129
① E 99
② C white
④ D 4
② G 3
④ C white
④ E 43
④ E 181
⑩ C 129
② E 65
② F 3
② E 176
③ C 161
④ F 59

STITCHES
① Japanese Ribbon Stitch
(page 131)
② Straight Stitch *(page 135)*
③ Lazy Daisy Stitch
(page 132)
④ French Knot Stitch
(page 130)
⑤ Feather Stitch *(page 128)*
⑥ Rouched Rose *(page 140)*
⑦ Buttonhole Stitch
(page 126)
⑧ Couching Stitch
(page 127)
⑨ Satin Stitch *(page 134)*
⑩ Stem Stitch *(page 134)*

FAUX FABERGÉ
and
FABULOUS

Exquisite Eggshell Floral Artistry

For fool-the eye replicas of Fabergé fineries, try your hand at embellishing ordinary goose eggs with silk ribbon embroidery. The Victorian hanging ornament shown here and the "eggstraordinary" projects on the following pages are all the inspiration of egg-decorating artisan, Joan Huff.

In the 23 years that Joan has been decorating eggs, she has traveled the world teaching and exhibiting her works of art. (She attends an average of nine egg shows a year in the United States alone!) Joan has used silk ribbon as an embellishment for her egg designs for quite some time, but only recently discovered that she could combine her childhood love of embroidery with her passion for transforming ordinary eggs into dazzling jewel boxes.

CUPID AND ROSES ORNAMENT

Send a message of love from cupid's bow in a very special form of greeting—an exquisite jeweled-egg lavishly embellished with silk ribbon embroidery! You can replicate Joan Huff's faux Fabergé ornament by referring to the Basic Egg Information on page 105.

In a hurry? Skip the hole-drilling phase by simply adding the small cupid print and then gluing purchased ribbon roses and trims in a pleasing arrangement as desired.

Spray paint the egg ivory and seal with a matte finish sealer. Glue a small cupid print to the center front of the egg. Following the drilling pattern, mark the design and drill holes on the egg as indicated. Following the pattern with the coded reference for stitches, materials, and colors, work the silk ribbon embroidery and embellish as desired.

MATERIALS

FABRIC
Plastic, papier maché, or real
   goose egg (See Sources.)

SILK EMBROIDERY RIBBON
5-yard (4.5m) reel of YLI 4-mm
   silk embroidery ribbon (**E**) in each
   of the following colors: green
   (32), dark red (50), light blue
   (124), brown (140), and rose (163)

ADDITIONAL MATERIALS
Dremel tool
Ivory spray paint
Mod Podge Matte Finish
Small cupid print
Tapestry needle - No. 24
Assorted gold trims, beads, and
   jewelry findings
Brass ornament stand

DRILLING PATTERN

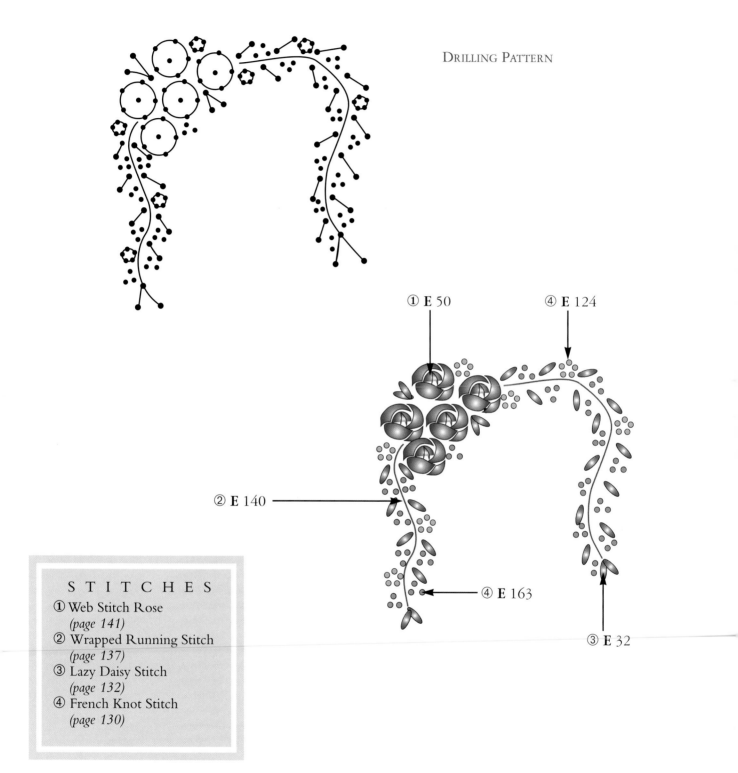

① **E** 50

④ **E** 124

② **E** 140

④ **E** 163

③ **E** 32

STITCHES
① Web Stitch Rose
(page 141)
② Wrapped Running Stitch
(page 137)
③ Lazy Daisy Stitch
(page 132)
④ French Knot Stitch
(page 130)

shown actual finished size

SILK RIBBON JEWEL BOX

Joan Huff's incredible jeweled egg box shown here is modeled after jewel-laden, turn-of-the-century eggs by Russian goldsmith, Peter Carl Fabergé. The large lattice-bordered goose egg is lined with braid-trimmed fabric, mounted on an ornate stand, and hinged to reveal a smaller chicken egg nestled inside. Both eggs are embellished with the web stitch rose and several other silk ribbon embroidery stitches.

When Joan designed this dramatic duo, she chose the web stitch rose for the coordinating floral theme. Three roses are clustered on the large egg while a single rose fits nicely on the smaller egg. As Joan points out to her students, it is extremely important to make sure the holes are drilled so that the roses will be centered on top of the egg. The position of the stems, leaves and buds can be adjusted as needed.

MATERIALS

FABRIC
Plastic, papier maché, or real
   goose egg; smaller nesting egg
   (See Sources.)

SILK EMBROIDERY RIBBON
5-yard (4.5m) reel of YLI 4-mm
   silk embroidery ribbon (**E**) in each
   of the following colors: dark green
   (21), brown (37), pink (111), and
   rose (112)

ADDITIONAL MATERIALS
Dremel tool
Ivory spray paint
Mod Podge Matte Finish
Epoxy
Tapestry needle - No. 24
Assorted gold trims, beads and
   jewelry findings
Small hinge
Filigree and marble base

DRILLING PATTERN

SMALL EGG

LARGE EGG

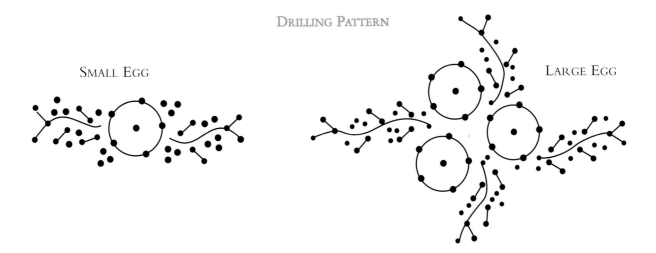

④ **E** 112

① **E** 111

③ **E** 21

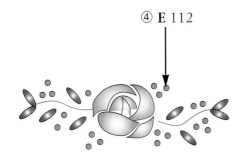

② **E** 37

S T I T C H E S
① Web Stitch Rose
   (page 141)
② Wrapped Running Stitch
   (page 137)
③ Lazy Daisy Stitch
   (page 132)
④ French Knot Stitch
   (page 130)

shown actual finished size

CINDERELLA'S COACH

When you've finished embellishing this fantasy floral masterpiece with silk ribbon embroidery, your friends will likely consider you the belle of the ball.

Taking center stage, Joan Huff's spectacular beaded coach is fashioned after

priceless museum originals by the famed Russian artist, Fabergé.

Amazingly enough, the heart-shaped hinged doors on either side of the coach swing out to enhance Cinderella's grand debut for an enchanted evening.

MATERIALS

FABRIC
Plastic, papier maché, or real
goose egg (See Sources.)

SILK EMBROIDERY RIBBON
5-yard (4.5m) reel of YLI 4-mm
silk embroidery ribbon (**E**)
in each of the following colors:
green (31), light blue (124),
dark rose (129), and pink (144)

ADDITIONAL MATERIALS
Dremel tool
Ivory spray paint
Mod Podge Matte Finish
Epoxy
AK Designs white pearls: 2mm
Tapestry needle - No. 24
Cinderella's coach-base and horses
(See Sources.)
Assorted gold trims, beads and
jewelry findings

DRILLING PATTERN FOR
LATTICE ON COACH

shown actual finished size

103

③ **E** 124

① **E** 144

③ **E** 129

② **E** 31

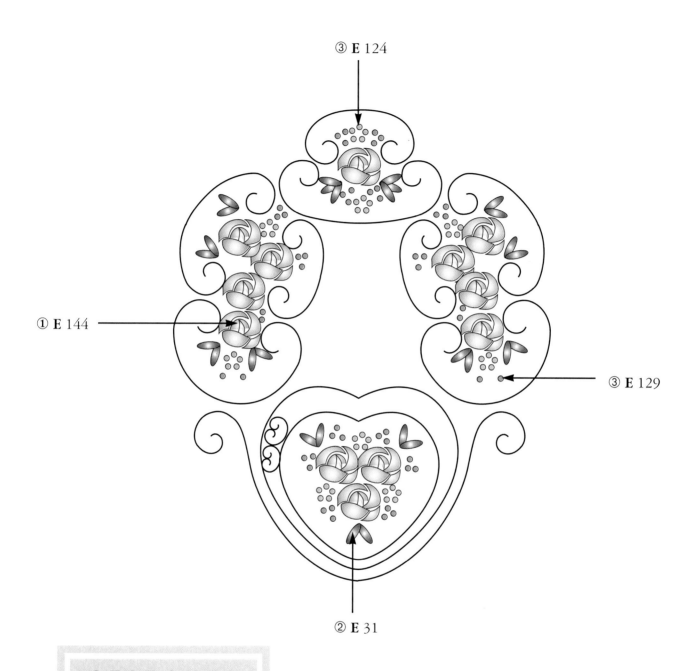

STITCHES
① Web Stitch Rose
(page 141)
② Lazy Daisy Stitch
(page 132)
③ French Knot Stitch
(page 130)

shown actual finished size

BASIC EGG INFORMATION

PREPARING THE EGG

- Divide egg into quarters and mark center girth. Trace drilling pattern on egg, and adjust placement of stems and leaves as necessary to compensate for size of egg.
- If egg will be a jewel box, glue hinge to lower half of egg with epoxy, if desired. Glue hinge to other half of egg when complete.
- Drill holes for stitching (marked by dots on drilling pattern).
- Cut lattice if applicable.
- Cut openings: (for the jewelry box, cut it into halves; for the coach, cut out the doors and windows; for the non-opening designs, cut a small oval from the back of egg to allow access to inside. Set oval aside and glue it back in place when embroidery is complete, trimming with cording to cover seams).
- Spray egg desired color.
- Spray with matte sealer.

EMBELLISHING THE EGG

- Bring the needle from the inside to the outside of the egg. Glue the tail of the ribbon in place on the inside of the egg. Do not glue over a hole in the egg. Work embroidery stitches.
- Use a short length of ribbon for stitching. (A long length of ribbon will fray from repeated pulling through holes drilled in egg.)
- Gently pull the ribbon through the egg, so as not to crack the egg.
- End off ribbon by pulling it to the inside of egg and gluing in place to secure.
- When all embroidery is complete, glue on gold cord, pearls, rhinestones or assorted jewelry findings to accent the design.

FINISHING THE INSIDE OF THE EGG

- Apply a thick coat of modeling paste to inside of egg over ribbon ends.
- Paint inside of egg.
- Coat with Mod Podge and apply Polyflakes.
- Line the inside base of the egg with fabric, trim as desired.
- Mount the completed egg on stand with epoxy.

Note: Additional tips and techniques for egg ornamentation, egg shows, classes, or commissioned eggs are available from the designer. (See Sources.)

HOLIDAY BRIGHTS

*Keepsake Gifts Stitched in Time
to Bloom for Christmas*

Making spirits bright will be a simple pleasure with a collection of
handcrafted gifts and decorating accents you can make in advance of
the oh-so-busy Christmas season.

Some of the projects shown here and on the following pages are
perfect for last-minute gifts; others can be made weeks ahead. Start
early with an elaborate embellished robe for a Victorian Father
Christmas and the floral heart insert for the jewelry box lid.

You'll still have plenty of time to make several small seasonal
sentiments like the NOEL satin stocking and poinsettia pin.

BARRETTE, BOX & FROSTED JAR

Lavishly embellished gifts are sophisticated reflections of the season when stitched on a rich burgundy background of silk Dupioni. With the revival of Victorian hearts and flowers in decorating themes, you'll find *these treasures welcomed by more than one grateful recipient. Or, better yet, make several sets and treat yourself to some holiday cheer!*

It's easy to treat everyone on your list to a heartwarming gift! The fabulous floral heart Esther designed for the lid insert of the jewelry box, shown in detail below, can be used as an imaginative embroidered silk ribbon accent for everything from a sweater or stocking to an ornament, pillow, or evening bag.

MATERIALS

FABRIC
1-10x15-inch (25.5x38-cm) piece of burgundy silk Dupioni for jewelry box top, 1-8x8-inch (20x20-cm) piece of burgundy silk Dupioni for frosted box top, and 1-5x8-inch (13x20-cm) piece of burgundy silk Dupioni for barrette

EMBROIDERY THREAD
YLI 601 fine metallic thread (**A**): Gold (GLD)
Kanagawa 1000 denier silk embroidery thread (**B**) in: dark teal green (731)

SILK EMBROIDERY RIBBON
5-yard (4.5m) reel of YLI 7-mm silk embroidery ribbon (**D**) in: dark red (50)
5-yard (4.5m) reel of YLI 4-mm silk embroidery ribbon (**E**) in each of the following colors: yellow (14), dark green (21), medium green (32), green (33), blue (44), burgundy (84), light lavender (101), lavender (102), aqua (116), periwinkle (118), and light blue (125)

ADDITIONAL MATERIALS
AK Designs seed beads: light blue (11/107), medium blue (11/105)
AK Designs large seed beads: red (6/709)
AK Designs 3mm gold metal beads
Beading monocord
Beading needle - No. 10
Chenille needle - No. 24 & No. 26
Crewel needle - No. 7
Milliner's needle -No. 7

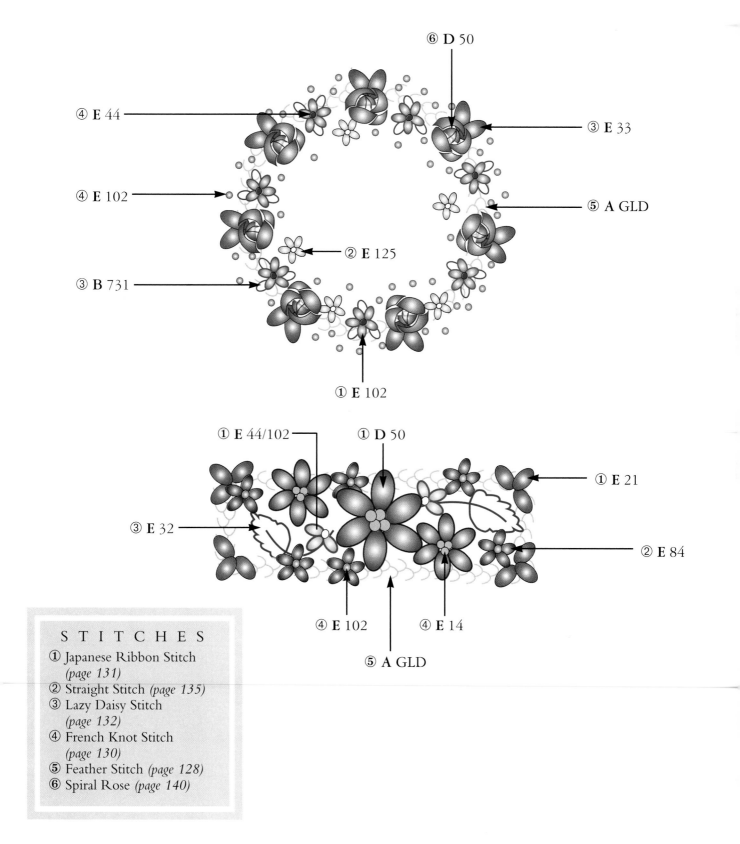

⑥ **D** 50

④ **E** 44

③ **E** 33

④ **E** 102

⑤ **A** GLD

② **E** 125

③ **B** 731

① **E** 102

① **E** 44/102

① **D** 50

① **E** 21

③ **E** 32

② **E** 84

④ **E** 102

④ **E** 14

⑤ **A** GLD

STITCHES
① Japanese Ribbon Stitch *(page 131)*
② Straight Stitch *(page 135)*
③ Lazy Daisy Stitch *(page 132)*
④ French Knot Stitch *(page 130)*
⑤ Feather Stitch *(page 128)*
⑥ Spiral Rose *(page 140)*

shown actual finished size

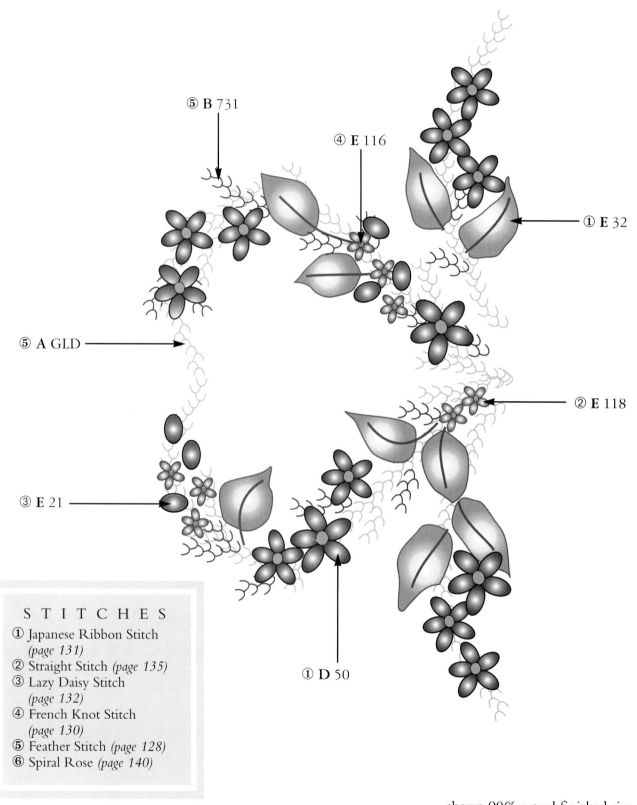

⑤ B 731

④ E 116

① E 32

⑤ A GLD

② E 118

③ E 21

① D 50

STITCHES
① Japanese Ribbon Stitch
(page 131)
② Straight Stitch *(page 135)*
③ Lazy Daisy Stitch
(page 132)
④ French Knot Stitch
(page 130)
⑤ Feather Stitch *(page 128)*
⑥ Spiral Rose *(page 140)*

shown 90% actual finished size

POINSETTIA PIN

MATERIALS

FABRIC
1- 5x5-inch (13x13-cm) piece of
dark green silk

SILK EMBROIDERY RIBBON
5-yard (4.5m) reel of YLI 7-mm
silk embroidery ribbon (**D**) in
each of the following colors:
red (49), and dark red (50)

5-yard (4.5m) reel of YLI 4-mm
silk embroidery ribbon (**E**) in each
of the following colors: gold (54),
and dark green (75)

ADDITIONAL MATERIALS
Chenille needle - No. 24
Crewel needle -   No. 7
Pin Backing

*Like many other
embroidery
enthusiasts, Esther
enjoys the challenge of
finding ways to use
every scrap of silk
ribbon. Looking much
like its summertime
sister—the dahlia—
this poinsettia works
up quickly when the
background petals are
worked in the under-
folded loop stitch.*

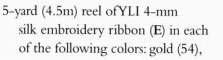

③ E 54

③ E 75

③ D 49

① D 50

② D 49

STITCHES
① Under-folded Loop
Stitch *(page 136)*
② Straight Stitch *(page 135)*
③ French Knot Stitch
(page 130)

SANTA'S HOODED CAPE

December is the month to pull out the decorating stops, and what could be more festive than Father Christmas displayed on the mantel or a tabletop. No matter what name you give him—Santa Claus, Saint Nicholas, Kriss Kringle—he's always in style at Christmas, especially in Esther Randall's home. As an avid collector, Esther is always looking for Santas to add to her extensive collection. She designed this replica of a Victorian Santa complete with a crazy patch coat and a unique hooded cape, embellished with silk ribbon embroidery and tied with tassels.

Discover how to crazy quilt in the mere twinkling of an eye—without ever having to piece a seam! On Santa's unique hooded cape, Esther used metallic gold feather stitches to divide the single piece of velvet into sections. The surprising result—crazy patch without all the piecing—was achieved in almost less time than it takes to say, "Merry Christmas!"

MATERIALS

FABRIC
1- 20x12-inch (51x30.5-cm) piece of velvet or taffeta

EMBROIDERY THREAD
YLI 601 fine metallic thread (**A**): Gold (GLD)
Kanagawa 1000 denier silk embroidery thread (**B**) in each of the following colors: gray blue (33), and spring green (165)

SILK EMBROIDERY RIBBON
5-yard (4.5m) reel of YLI 7-mm silk embroidery ribbon (**D**) in each of the following colors: green (32), and dark red (50)

5-yard (4.5m) reel of YLI 4-mm silk embroidery ribbon (**E**) in each of the following colors: yellow (14), green (32), purple (102), and periwinkle (117)

ADDITIONAL MATERIALS
AK Designs large seed beads: red (6/709)
Beading monocord
Beading needle - No. 10
Chenille needle - No. 24
Crewel needle - No. 7
Between needle - No. 10

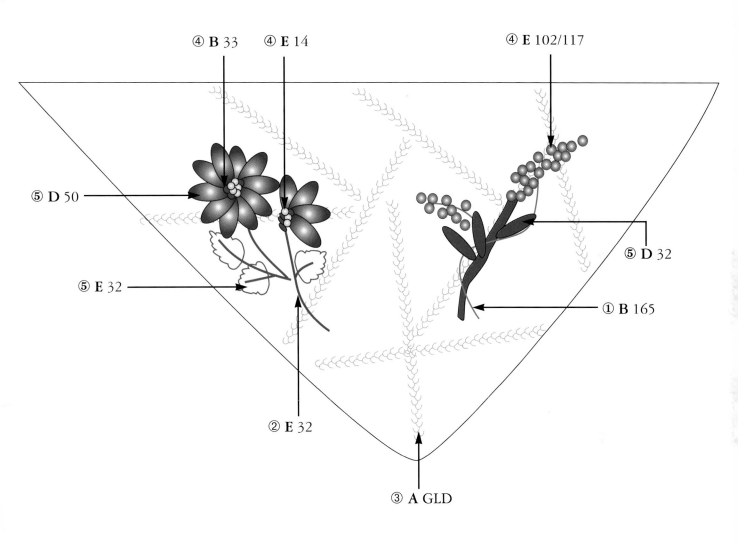

④ B 33 ④ E 14 ④ E 102/117

⑤ D 50

⑤ E 32

② E 32

⑤ D 32

① B 165

③ A GLD

STITCHES
① Chain Stitch *(page 127)*
② Couching Stitch
   (page 127)
③ Feather Stitch *(page 128)*
④ French Knot Stitch
   (page 130)
⑤ Japanese Ribbon Stitch
   (page 131)

shown 55% actual finished size

NOEL SATIN STOCKING

Seasonal accents and a holiday greeting are a joyful combination when worked in silk ribbon embroidery on this embellished satin stocking designed, appropriately enough, by needle artist Merry Nader.

The vivid jewel tones of the silk ribbon embroidery provide a stunning contrast to the snowy white satin background on a Victorian-inspired stocking sure to become a treasured holiday heirloom.

Merry Nader's embellishing on the stocking demonstrates another interesting effect that can be achieved with silk ribbon. The stripes on the ornament depicted on the stocking and across the stocking's toe are both simply long straight stitches of ribbon with either herringbone stitches or French knots of Kanagawa Embroidery Thread on top to secure them.

MATERIALS

FABRIC
1- 10x12-inch (25.5x30.5-cm) piece of white satin

EMBROIDERY THREAD
Kanagawa 1000 denier silk embroidery thread (**B**) in each of the following colors: cranberry (6), purple (22), green (113), violet (117), teal green (138), dark purple (144), gray green (157), salmon (177), and eggplant (819)

SILK EMBROIDERY RIBBON
5-yard (4.5m) reel of YLI 7-mm silk embroidery ribbon (**D**) in each of the following colors: pink (8), dark green (21), red (48), and antique purple (177)

5-yard (4.5m) reel of YLI 4-mm silk embroidery ribbon (**E**) in each of the following colors: gold (53), bright pink (152), olive green (171), apricot (172), and antique violet (177)

ADDITIONAL MATERIALS
Chenille needle - No. 24
Crewel needle -   No. 7

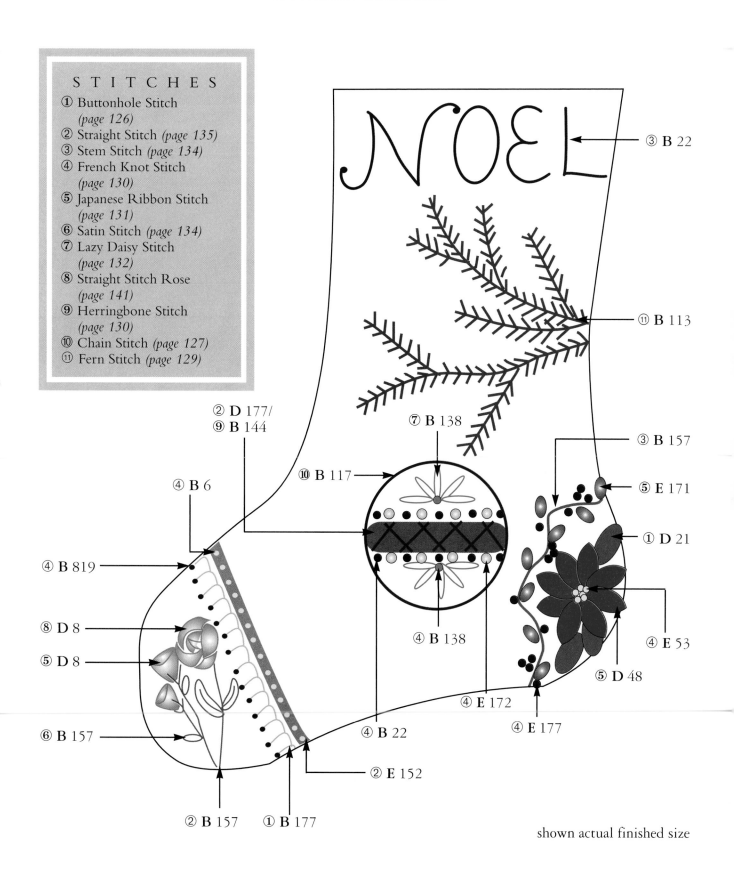

STITCHES
① Buttonhole Stitch
   (page 126)
② Straight Stitch *(page 135)*
③ Stem Stitch *(page 134)*
④ French Knot Stitch
   (page 130)
⑤ Japanese Ribbon Stitch
   (page 131)
⑥ Satin Stitch *(page 134)*
⑦ Lazy Daisy Stitch
   (page 132)
⑧ Straight Stitch Rose
   (page 141)
⑨ Herringbone Stitch
   (page 130)
⑩ Chain Stitch *(page 127)*
⑪ Fern Stitch *(page 129)*

③ B 22

⑪ B 113

② D 177/
⑨ B 144

⑦ B 138

③ B 157

⑩ B 117

⑤ E 171

④ B 6

① D 21

④ B 819

④ B 138

④ E 53

⑧ D 8

⑤ D 8

⑤ D 48

⑥ B 157

④ E 172

④ E 177

④ B 22

② E 152

② B 157   ① B 177

shown actual finished size

117

QUICK-
STITCHED
by
MACHINE

Overnight Sensations

For last-minute gifts and quick trims for fashions and

accessories, time is on your side when you use your sewing

machine to add simple embroidered embellishments.

Several of the major sewing machine manufacturers have

developed techniques for easy embroidery by machine. On the

following pages a leading designer for each contributes an

original design that has been quick-stitched by machine, and

shares special tips and techniques to help you get started.

The evening bag shown here was designed by Judith Kurth

for Pfaff. (Please turn the page for instructions.) Use the

designers' inspirations for creating your own spectacular quick-

stitched silk ribbon embroidery embellishments—and yours,

too, can be made with time to spare!

EVENING BAG

*Silk ribbon is a
natural when
combined with
machine embroidery.
Work the machine
embroidery first to
create the leaves on
the handbag, and
then embellish with
silk ribbon and
beads.*

*Basic black taffeta provides a striking
background for the intricate embroidered
leaves and dimensional roses worked in pink
silk ribbon by machine.*

*Designer and educator, Judith Kurth,
stitched her impressive floral design on an
elegant, drawstring evening bag trimmed
with braided cording, using attachments for
the Pfaff sewing machine.*

STITCHES
① Machine Embroidery
② Loop Stitches
③ French Knot Stitch

MATERIALS

FABRIC
Black taffeta

SILK EMBROIDERY RIBBON
5-yard (4.5m) reel of YLI 7-mm
    silk embroidery ribbon (**D**) in:
    pink (144)
5-yard (4.5m) reel of YLI 4-mm
    silk embroidery ribbon (**E**) in
    each of the following colors:
    green (32), and pink (68)

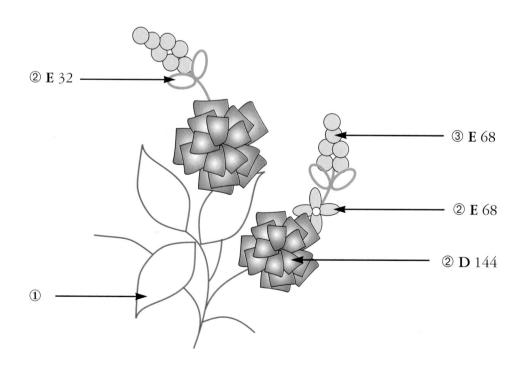

② **E** 32

③ **E** 68

② **E** 68

② **D** 144

①

shown actual finished size

MACHINE SILK RIBBON EMBROIDERY

MACHINE SET UP:
- Place the feed dogs down and put your machine in the darning position. Remove the sewing foot and insert a #80 regular needle. Thread your machine with invisible nylon thread and loosen the top thread tension to around #4. (If you still see bobbin thread coming to the top of your work, loosen the top thread tension some more.) Place YLI Lingerie or Mettler 60 weight thread in the bobbin.

GENERAL WORKING ORDER:
- Work leaves first.
- Sew flowers over leaves to hide ends of the ribbon.
- Add beads last by machine or hand.

PETALS AND LEAVES:
- Take a few tiny stitches in the fabric to secure the thread.
- Lay the silk ribbon over the stitches with the needle behind the ribbon; sew over the end of the ribbon to secure. Trim ends of ribbon.
- Sew to the end of the leaf or petal without sewing through ribbon; curve the ribbon and tack in place, sew back to the base of the leaf or petal.
- Sew over end of the ribbon.
- Repeat as necessary for additional leaves or petals.

FRENCH KNOTS:
- Take a few tiny stitches in the fabric to secure the thread.
- Lay the silk ribbon over the stitches with the needle behind the ribbon; sew over the end of the ribbon to secure. Trim ends of ribbon.
- Thread the loose end of the ribbon into a tapestry needle.
- Wrap the ribbon around the machine needle one or two times.
- Insert the tapestry needle at the top of the wrapped ribbon and out through the bottom.
- Gently pull the ribbon to form a knot; sew over the ribbon next to the knot to secure.

ROSES:
- Take a few tiny stitches in the fabric to secure the thread.
- Lay the silk ribbon in the center of the drawn circle; sew over the end of the ribbon to secure.
- Attach a bead or pearl in the center of the rose.
- Make loops around the pearl in a counter-clockwise direction, attaching as you go.
- Sew ribbon ends through the fabric with a large-eyed needle and secure on wrong side.

CHILD'S VEST

Silk ribbon embellishments add even greater dimensional impact when worked on a machine-embroidered denim vest. Judy Nowicki, an educator and talented designer, uses the attachments on her Viking sewing machine to work both the machine embroidery and the silk ribbon embroidery.

Judy has created numerous quick-stitched by machine projects, including fashions for The Art of Sewing series, modeled by Sue Hausmann on her nationally televised program—America Sews.

MATERIALS

FABRIC
Purchased denim vest

SILK EMBROIDERY RIBBON
5-yard (4.5m) reel of YLI 4-mm silk embroidery ribbon (**E**) in each of the following colors: white (3), pink (8), and green (21)

To make a fun vest covered with apples from the teacher, Judy suggests that you work the machine embroidery first, randomly spacing the hearts, apples, and the large leaves.

Following the pattern with the coded reference for stitches, materials, and colors, work the ribbon embroidered flowers and leaves in clusters adjoining the machine embroidered motifs. Adjust the placement as necessary to work with your machine embroidery. The roses are given a special touch by working a white rose and then completing it with several pink petals.

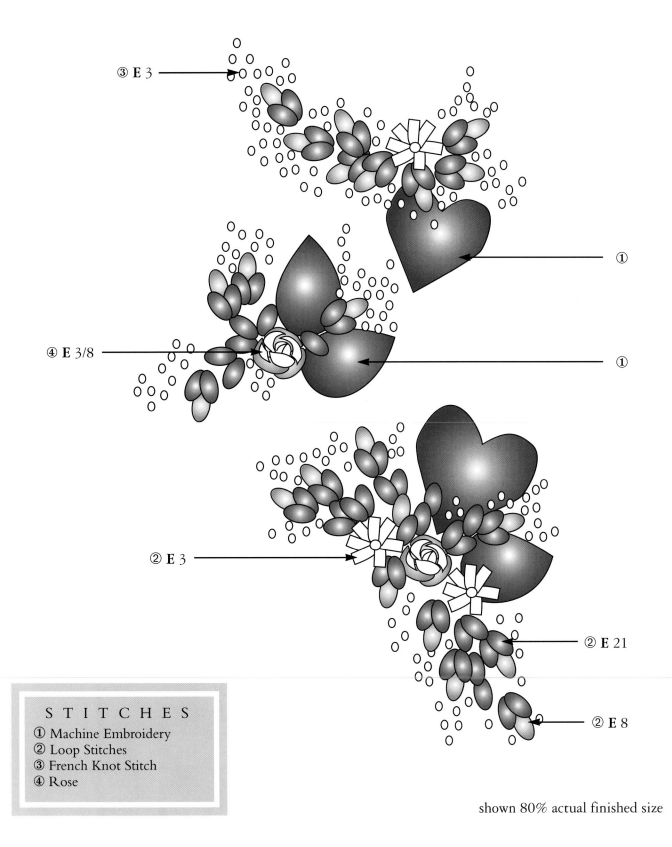

③ **E** 3

④ **E** 3/8

② **E** 3

①

①

② **E** 21

② **E** 8

S T I T C H E S
① Machine Embroidery
② Loop Stitches
③ French Knot Stitch
④ Rose

shown 80% actual finished size

POCKETFUL-OF-POSIES

Fresh accents for your favorite chambray shirt will bloom overnight when you quick-stitch them by machine. Designer and educator, Patsy Shields, has cleverly done just that using the attachments for her Baby Lock sewing machine. On the inset photo below, note that the roses are stitched between the buttons directly onto the placket.

MATERIALS

FABRIC
Purchased chambray shirt

SILK EMBROIDERY RIBBON
5-yard (4.5m) reel of YLI 7-mm
    silk embroidery ribbon (**D**) in:
    blue (44)
5-yard (4.5m) reel of YLI 4-mm
    silk embroidery ribbon (**E**) in
    each of the following colors:
    yellow (14), green (33), pink
    (152), and burgundy (181)

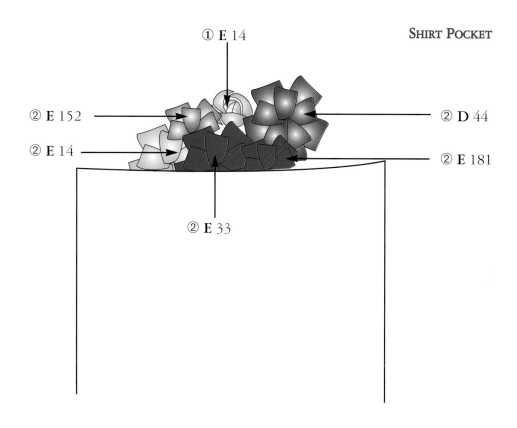

① E 14

② E 152

② D 44

② E 14

② E 181

② E 33

① E 181

PLACKET TRIM

STITCHES
① Rose
② Loop Stitches

shown actual finished size

STEP-BY-STEP GUIDE TO THE STITCHES

BULLION TIPPED LAZY DAISY STITCH

This stitch makes a beautiful petal with soft angles—perfect for flowers such as the tulip, lily of the valley and fuchsia.

1. Bring the needle up at A. Pierce the fabric at B and then at C without pulling it through either stitch.

2. Wrap the ribbon around the needle from left to right two full wraps.

3. With the thumb of your left hand holding the wraps secure, pull the needle through gently. Angle the stitch to the right and pierce into the fabric to secure the stitch so it lays on the fabric at D.

Note: To create a complete tulip, work a second stitch (wrapping the needle from right to left) directly to the left of the first stitch.

Pierce at D to the far left. The center petal of the flower is simply a Japanese ribbon stitch.

BUTTONHOLE STITCH

This is an excellent outlining stitch. When worked in a circle it becomes a flower. It is the perfect choice in irregular areas for effects such as leaves.

1. To make the stitch, bring your needle and ribbon up through the fabric at A. Hold the ribbon flat against the fabric at point A and to the left, with your left thumb. Go down at B and up at C, always keeping the ribbon under the needle.

2. With the next stitch, point C becomes point A and you repeat the original stitch.

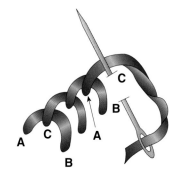

CHAIN STITCH

1. To begin working the chain stitch, bring the needle up at A.

2 Holding the ribbon against the fabric with your left thumb, form a loop with the ribbon from A to B.

3. Insert the needle at B and bring it up at C with one motion, making sure that the ribbon is underneath the point of the needle, and does not twist as it comes through at C.

Note: The distance from A to B should be close enough to ensure the appearance of a chain, since each individual stitch forms a link in the chain. As you begin the next stitch, C becomes A and you repeat the stitch, making as many links as you need for the length of the chain desired.

COUCHING STITCH

This stitch is used to apply ribbon, thread, braid, or other embellishments to the fabric when these embellishments are too large to stitch in the traditional manner. A single long stitch is made and then tacked down with another ribbon or thread. Couching is the attaching or tacking of the embellishment to the fabric. The tacking stitch can be perpendicular to the couched decoration or slanted, depending on the desired appearance. The tacking ribbon or thread may be the same color or a contrasting color.

1. The couching stitch is made by bringing the threaded needle up at A and down at B. Pull the tacking thread or ribbon tight, thereby holding the decoration to the fabric.

2. Repeat the stitch until you have completely attached the decoration.

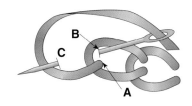

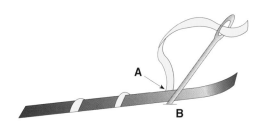

CROSS STITCH

The cross stitch is a series of straight stitches combined to make a pattern of "Xs."

1. Bring your needle and ribbon up at A, down at B, up at C, and down at D.
2. Repeat, making sure that the stitch from C to D is over the stitch from A to B in every "X" you create.

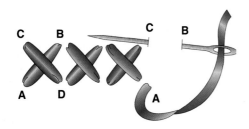

FEATHER STITCH

Before you begin this stitch, imagine a straight line on the fabric that runs in the center of the leaf or other pattern you are stitching. This imaginary line serves as a guide as you sew individual stitches on either side of it.

1. Starting at the top of the imaginary line, bring the needle up through the fabric at A and down at B, holding the ribbon loose on top of the fabric with your left thumb to form a loop from A to B. Allow the ribbon to curve gently, but not twist.
2. Come up at C, keeping the ribbon under the needle. This is the point of the "V" formed by the ribbon from A to B.

Note: Be careful not to pull the stitch so tightly that it compresses and distorts. A to B to C forms the individual stitch that is alternated on each side of the imaginary line. As you begin each individual stitch, keep in mind that C of the previous stitch becomes A for the next stitch.

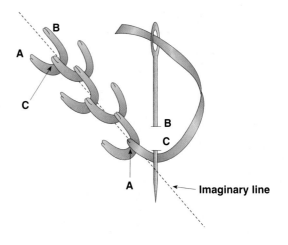

FERN STITCH

The fern stitch consists of three straight stitches all of equal length and all focusing at the same point (A to B, C to A, and D to A).

1. First, bring your needle and ribbon up at A, down at B, up at C and down at A, up at D and down at A.

2. Repeat this same series of stitches over and over to form the next and continuing fern leaves and stems.

Note: The fern line may be straight or curved.

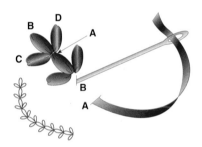

FISHBONE STITCH

The fishbone stitch is simply two sharply slanted flat stitches that cross each other between two parallel imaginary lines. Work from left to right.

1. Bring your ribbon and needle up at A, hold it flat to the fabric, go down at B, up at C and down at D. Notice that C is perpendicular to (directly across from) A. B is also perpendicular to D.

2. Repeat these stitches to complete the distance or area you are covering, always keeping the ribbon flat.

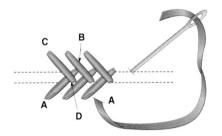

Note: The distance between A and D and C and B where the needle enters should be consistent with each consecutive stitch.

FLY STITCH

This stitch is similar to both the lazy daisy and the feather stitch.

1. Bring the needle up at A. Hold the ribbon flat on the fabric with your left thumb.

2. Take the needle down at B and up at C in one stitch. Notice that the ribbon from A to B forms a loop. The stitch from C to D goes over the ribbon and holds the ribbon in place, making the stitch look like a "V."

Note: The fly stitch is good for a variety of uses including buds on a stem, birds in flight, butterflies, or an attractive border.

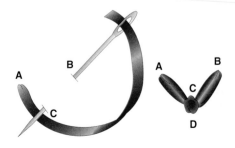

FRENCH KNOT STITCH

The French knot is easy and fun to make.

1. Bring the needle and ribbon up at A. Pull the ribbon taut with your left hand. Wrap the ribbon around the needle once, keeping it flat. More wraps will make a larger knot.

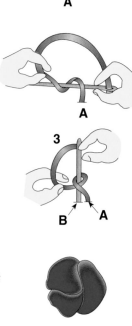

2. Insert the needle at B and pull the ribbon so the knot is pushed close to the fabric. Keep the tension even, but do not pull too tightly or you will be unable to pull the needle through the knot and the fabric. And, if you leave the ribbon too loose an unwanted loop will appear at the knot.

3. Pull the ribbon down at B. Keep holding the ribbon taut until most of the ribbon has been pulled through. Notice that as you pull the ribbon all the way through, it gives the appearance of water going down a drain.

HERRINGBONE STITCH

This stitch is a line of overlapping crosses or "Xs." It is a popular stitch that is easy and fun to make.

1. Stitch from left to right, bringing your needle and ribbon up at A.

2. With the ribbon flat, go down at B and up at C in one stitch. Now, cross over the ribbon that runs from A to B and insert your needle at D, bringing it up at the next A in one stitch.

3. Repeat these stitches, forming a series of "Xs" or crosses. The location and size of each cross is determined by the distance between B and C and between A and D.

Note: The difference between the herringbone stitch and the cross stitch is that the crossing of the ribbon alternates from top to bottom in the herringbone stitch and is always in the center of the stitches in the cross stitch.

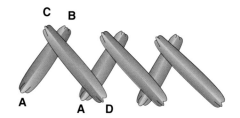

JAPANESE RIBBON STITCH

This stitch is similar to a running or straight stitch with the advantage that it allows for very accurate placement of the ribbon and gives a curled effect to one end of the stitch. This stitch makes extraordinary leaves and petals.

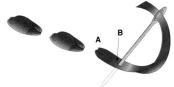

1. Bring your needle up at A. Hold the ribbon flat, exactly where it will be stitched to the fabric.

2. Insert the needle back through the ribbon at B, which is in the center of the width of the ribbon. You will pull the ribbon down through itself. Tighten the ribbon slowly. Curls will form on each side of the ribbon. Watch the curling until it forms the appearance you want. The length of the curl depends on how tightly you pull the ribbon through at B. If you want a raised and puffed appearance, leave the ribbon from A to B loose. (Piercing the ribbon close to the left edge will allow the stitch to curve to the left;

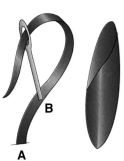

piercing the ribbon close to the right edge will allow the stitch to curve to the right.) Two or three small Japanese ribbon stitches originating from the same place and fanning out slightly

make a delightful small bud, especially when tiny green stitches are added at the base of the Japanese stitches.

3. To create two-tone petals or leaves, thread two lengths of silk ribbon through the needle treating them as one ribbon. Keep the ribbon smooth and flat. Tie a knot at the end of the pair of ribbons. Make your stitch from A to B with the main color on top so that the opposite color forms the resulting curl at the end of the stitch.

4. To create two-tone petals showing a larger area of each color, bring the needle up at A, separate the ribbons slightly, matching the right edge of one ribbon with the left edge of the other. Go down at B, where the ribbons meet in the center, piercing both ribbons along the adjoining edges.

LAZY DAISY STITCH

This is simply a separate single chain stitch. Instead of the next chain holding down the loop, a small stitch secures it. Keep the silk ribbon untwisted and full when stitching.

1. Bring the ribbon up at A. Hold the ribbon flat against the fabric with your thumb while forming the loop. Insert the needle through

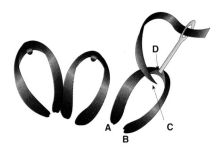

the fabric at B and bring the needle up at C in the same stitch. Pull the ribbon through, keeping the loop full and puffy. Pierce the top edge of the loop at D and pull through. This will secure the lazy daisy from shifting.

2. To create the look of quilled paper, or to add additional height to the stitch, work the basic lazy daisy stitch, from A to B. Allow the ribbon to stand on edge on the fabric. Bring the needle up at C in the formed loop. Pierce the bottom edge of the ribbon loop at D.

Note: Other options include securing the loop of the lazy daisy stitch with a French knot or Japanese ribbon stitch.

LOOPED PETAL STITCH

1. To make this stitch, bring the ribbon up at A, holding the ribbon to form a loop, with one half of the ribbon on top of the other half of the ribbon. Hold the loop with your left thumb so that the ribbon folds back evenly. Do not have any twist in the ribbon or you will lose the petal effect.

2. Insert the needle at B, pulling the ribbon until it forms the petal length and appearance you want. Make several of these stitches to form flower petals.

3. The center of the flowers may be a French knot or a straight stitch. Either stitch must be stitched at the base of each petal to secure the petals to the fabric.

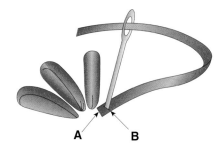

RIBBON LOOP STITCH

The ribbon loop stitch creates a series of overlapping loops that can give a unique appearance to your design, depending upon the puffiness of the loops.

1. Bring your needle and ribbon up at A. Hold the ribbon against the fabric so that it is flat or looped, depending on the desired puffiness for each stitch.

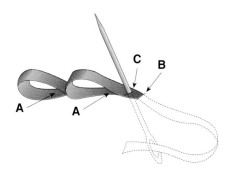

2. Insert your needle at B and up at C, which is through the center of the width of the ribbon. Pull the ribbon through until it is tight and holding the loop in place. Repeat the stitch until you have the length of the overlapping loops you need in your design or pattern.

RUNNING STITCH

1. Bring the needle up at A from the underside of the fabric. Insert the needle in and out of the fabric as in general sewing, taking several stitches at the same time (for example: basting seams or quilting).

Note: The individual stitches can be longer on top than underneath or spaced evenly. Longer stitches look flatter than the short stitches. Keep your stitches straight on top by bringing them through the fabric evenly, giving the stitch a smooth appearance. You are the artist— use the stitch length that is most attractive and appealing to you.

SATIN STITCH

The satin stitch is a series of straight stitches done side by side to completely cover a specified area. The stitch is most beautiful when it is uniform and smooth. It is ideal for filling odd-shaped spaces and curved areas.

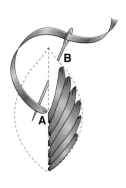

1. Bring the needle up at A, then down at B. This completes one stitch. Keep the ribbon flat, making sure that each stitch is close to, but not overlapping, the previous stitch. The distance from A to B is variable for each stitch, depending on the space or the area you are interested in covering.

STEM STITCH

This stitch is a basic embroidery stitch. It is ideal for outlining and may be used any place where a single line is desired. Rows of stem stitches make good filler for large areas.

1. Begin the stitch by bringing your needle up at A. Hold the ribbon flat on the fabric with your thumb to either side of the stem line. Regardless of which side you choose to begin your stitching, remember to stay on the same side with the rest of your stitches.

2. The stitch from A to B is a single stem stitch and is repeated as many times as is needed for the length of the stem.

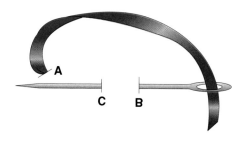

Note: Notice that the beginning of the second stitch C and every stitch thereafter begins halfway back in the preceding stitch and on the same side of the ribbon each time.

STRAIGHT STITCH

This is a simple, flat stitch from A to B. Its length is variable, depending upon the appearance and desired results.

STRAIGHT STITCH WITH FRENCH KNOT

This stitch is a straight stitch with a French knot at the end of it.

1. Bring the ribbon up A and insert it at B, making sure you keep the ribbon flat on top by holding it firmly against the fabric with your left thumb.
2. Bring your needle up through the center of the width of the ribbon at point C. Make a French knot by wrapping and inserting the needle at D, which is very close to C. The distance from B to C should be close enough that the completed knot is located at the end of the flat stitch.

Note: The length of your flat stitch is variable, depending on the desired effect.

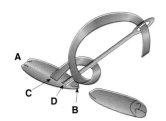

TWISTED LAZY DAISY STITCH

Normally, when stitching with silk ribbon you want the ribbon to be flat as you work with it on the fabric surface. However, often when a flower first opens, some of the petals are curled and not fully open.

1. To achieve that curled appearance when using the lazy daisy stitch for flower petals, twist the ribbon several times after you bring it up at A.
2. Insert the needle at B, while holding the curled ribbon in a loop shape. Pull the ribbon through C slowly to form a curled petal appearance.
3. Insert the needle at D to tack the looped ribbon to the fabric. This stitch is pretty as the center of a flower.

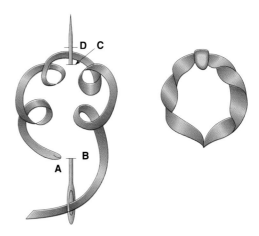

TWISTED STRAIGHT STITCH

This stitch is the same as the straight stitch, except that you twist the ribbon before inserting the needle down at B. The number of twists and the length of the stitch gives a variety of finished results.

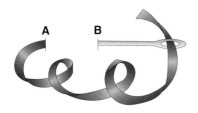

UNDER-FOLDED LOOP STITCH

The under-folded loop stitch is another approach used for creating petals.

1. Come up through the fabric at A. Keeping the ribbon flat, fold the ribbon under and to the right at a 45° angle. Use a pin to hold the point of the loop C.

2. Fold the ribbon over and down toward the starting point. Insert the needle into the ribbon at B, just beside the starting point A, so that the ribbon at B slightly overlaps.

3. Now, go back to point C where the ribbon was folded and pinned. Make a few tiny stitches to secure the point at C.

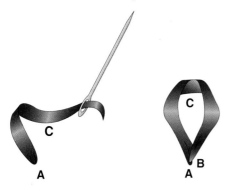

VICTORIAN STACKING STITCH

This stitch is an expanded herringbone stitch.

1. Make the herringbone stitch the distance you want it to cover. Expand the distance between the crossed points to allow room to add additional herringbone stitches.

2. Place the second set beside the first series of herringbone stitches. Each series of herringbone stitches may be completed with different colors of ribbon, creating an interesting stacked effect.

WOVEN RIBBON STITCH

The beauty of silk ribbon is highlighted in this stitch, since it may be used to create a basket or container for a bouquet of silk flowers. The stitch is perfect as a smooth surface and may be sewn at right angles or offset. It is a good choice for covering a large area in a solid color or for working a raised, stuffed area.

1. To begin the stitch, sew several straight stitches close together, as you do with the satin stitch. Allow these stitches to have a slight amount of give. Make an uneven number of straight stitches.

2. Then with either the same color ribbon or a contrasting color, weave in and out of the straight stitches. Be sure to alternate rows so that the woven effect is evident.

Note: Do not stitch into the fabric except at the edge of your weaving where you go back into the fabric to secure the ribbon you are weaving.

WRAPPED RUNNING STITCH

Complete the length of running stitches you need. The running stitches don't need to be flat because they will be wrapped and unseen. The line of your running stitches may be straight or curved.

1. Begin wrapping the running stitches at the last running stitch you made (C).

2. Wrap each individual running stitch, keeping the ribbon flat as you wrap. When wrapping, do not stitch through the fabric.

Note: Wrapping consists of going under and over each running stitch in succession from right to left until you have wrapped all of the running stitches. At the end of the wrapping, pierce into the fabric at D and either tie off or continue with a new stitch.

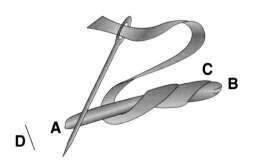

ROSE STITCHES

BULLION ROSE

A bullion rose is simply a cluster of individual bullion knots.

1. Begin by bringing the needle up at A. Put the needle through the fabric from B and then back to A again. Do not pull the needle through the fabric.

2. Keeping the ribbon flat, wrap the tip of the needle evenly until an area is covered that is approximately equal to the length of the bullion you desire.

3. Hold the wraps of ribbon secure with the thumb and forefinger of your left hand. Slowly draw the needle through, until the knot lies flat on the fabric. Insert the needle back through the fabric next to B.

4. To make a rose, work a single bullion knot wrapping the needle five to nine times. Work two more bullion knots one above, and one below the first, allowing them to gently surround the center of the rose.

CHAIN STITCH ROSE

The simple chain stitch can be used to create a rather fancy rose.

1. Begin with a single chain stitch in the center and continue stitching additional chain stitches in a tight spiral.

2. When the rose is of the desired size, tack down the last chain stitch with a single stitch.

3. Place French knots in the center or use beads for a special effect.

COUCHED STITCH ROSE

To achieve the best results when making a couched stitch rose, leave fullness in the ribbon between couching stitches. The fuller the ribbon, the more beautiful the rose. Be sure to couch in a very tight spiral so that no fabric shows.

FRENCH KNOT ROSE

To form the French knot rose, use all sizes of silk ribbon.

1. Make a single French knot. When twisting the ribbon around the needle to form the French knot, give the ribbon plenty of loop. Then as you pull the ribbon back through the fabric, pull it slowly to keep it loose. Watch the shape of the rose form. When you have the rose appearance you want, simply stop pulling the ribbon through the fabric.

2. Secure the knot on the underside. These French knot roses may be sewn in clusters.

LAZY DAISY AND STRAIGHT STITCH ROSE

1. To embroider this rose, first make a lazy daisy stitch using wide ribbon (7mm or 13mm).

2. At the beginning of the lazy daisy stitch (A), and to the left, place a straight stitch that overlaps the left side of the lazy daisy stitch, as shown in the diagram.

3. Next, place another straight stitch to the right, overlapping the preceding straight stitch and on the right side of the lazy daisy stitch, thus forming a simple rose.

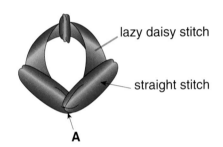

lazy daisy stitch

straight stitch

A

ROUCHED ROSE

To make an elegant rouched rose, begin with any size ribbon.

1. Pull a single header thread A along an edge of the ribbon to gather it.
2. With a needle and thread, start at the center of the flower (you choose the size) curve and tack the ribbon along the gathered edge, spiraling and overlapping it to form a rose. When you have achieved the desired-size rose, clip the ribbon, pierce the fabric, and then with your next stitch secure the raw edges of the ribbon.

SPIRAL ROSE

1. Bring the ribbon up through the fabric at A (the center of your rose), spiraling and twisting it into a soft tube shape.

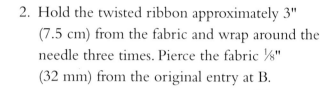

2. Hold the twisted ribbon approximately 3" (7.5 cm) from the fabric and wrap around the needle three times. Pierce the fabric ⅛" (32 mm) from the original entry at B.

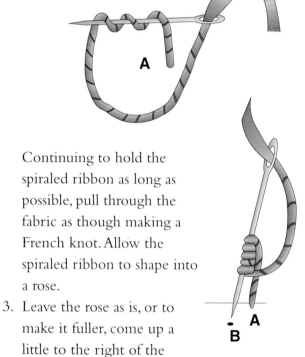

Continuing to hold the spiraled ribbon as long as possible, pull through the fabric as though making a French knot. Allow the spiraled ribbon to shape into a rose.

3. Leave the rose as is, or to make it fuller, come up a little to the right of the original starting point. Twist the ribbon gently and curve halfway around the base of the rose.
4. Continue adding petals overlapping them slightly as you go until the desired fullness is achieved. Use a needle and thread in a matching color to tack through the center of the rose to further secure.
5. When working leaves, pierce outer petals of the rose with Japanese ribbon stitches, lazy daisy stitches or straight stitches to secure.

STRAIGHT STITCH ROSE

1. Begin with a loose French knot at the center of the flower.
2. Add straight stitches around the French knot, each one partially covering the previous stitch. With each stitch, pierce the bottom edge of the previous stitch to keep it from covering the center of the rose. Several rows will make a nice-sized rose.
3. Secure the last straight stitch on top of the fabric with a tiny stitch. Place a lazy daisy stitch as a leaf beside the rose covering the tiny tacking stitch just made.

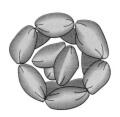

WEB STITCH ROSE

1. Work an eyelet stitch with Kanagawa 1000 denier silk embroidery thread. Bring the needle up at A, down at B, up at C, back down at B. Continue to work the spokes of the eyelet D, E, and F always putting the needle down in the center common hole B.

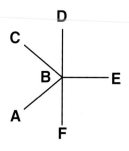

2. To make the rose, with silk ribbon begin at the center of the eyelet stitch at B. Wrap the ribbon over and under the spokes. Keep the ribbon flat.

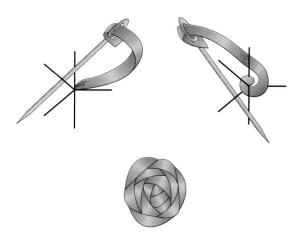

WRAPPED STRAIGHT STITCH ROSE

1. Make a single straight stitch at the center of the rose, bringing the needle back up at the beginning point.
2. Wrap the stitch several times to get the thickness you desire keeping the ribbon flat. Do not stitch into the fabric until the wrapping is complete. Then, pierce the fabric to secure the wrapped stitch before starting your next stitch.
3. Continue making straight stitches, wrapping and securing each one separately. Arrange each of those wrapped straight stitches so they form a rose shape.

SOURCES

Note: Silk embroidery thread and ribbon for all the projects—YLI Corporation, P.O. Box 109, Provo, UT 84603; 800/854-1932.

Chapter One: Pattern for girl's party dress—Butterick No. 5321, sizes 8–16.

Dupioni 100% handwoven silk—LOGANTEX, available retail through the Stitching Corner, 480 Freedom Blvd., Provo, UT 84601; 801/374-1200.

Pattern for girl's smocked dress—CHILDREN'S CORNER, No. 200 (Olivia), sizes 1–12, available retail through the Stitching Corner, 480 Freedom Blvd., Provo, UT 84601; 801/374-1200.

Pattern for pieced vest—PEACE CREEK, No. 18, sizes small, medium, large, available retail through the Stitching Corner, 480 Freedom Blvd., Provo, UT 84601; 801/374-1200.

Pattern for crazy quilt vest—FOUR CORNERS, No. 5000 (The Invest), available retail through the Stitching Corner, 480 Freedom Blvd., Provo, UT 84601; 801/374-1200.

Chapter Two: Precut ivory afghan—CHARLES CRAFT, available retail.

Chapter Three: Ribbons for afghan fringe—YLI Corporation, P.O. Box 109, Provo, UT 84603; 800/854-1932.

Chapter Four: Laptop stationery desk—THE BOMBAY COMPANY, P.O. Box 161009, Ft. Worth, TX 76161-1009; 800/829-7789.

Seed beads for jar lids—AK Designs beads available from Beadiak, 29350 Pacific Coast Hwy, #2A, Malibu, CA 90265, 800/521-2525.

Heart embroidery kit—YLI Corporation, P.O. Box 109, Provo, UT 84603, 800/854-1932.

Seed beads for pillow—AK Designs beads available from Beadiak, 29350 Pacific Coast Hwy, #2A, Malibu, CA 90265, 800/521-2525.

Glove and scarf box—available retail through Creative Furnishings, 12357 Saraglen Dr., Saratoga, CA 95070; 408/996-7745 *OR* Tomorrow's Treasures, Inc., 19722 144th Ave., N.E., Woodinville, WA 98072; 206/487-2636.

Treasure Box Cottage—MARY JANE COLLECTION, TIR-Y-FRON LANE, Pontybodkin, Mold, CLWYD, CH7, 4TU, United Kingdom; *OR* YLI Corporation, P.O. Box 109, Provo, UT 84603; 800/854-1932.

Chapter Five: Ribbon roses "by the yard" trim—YLI Corporation, P.O. Box 109, Provo, UT 84603; 800/854-1932.

Decorative pin backs—YLI Corporation, P.O. Box 109, Provo, UT 84603, 800/854-1932.

Chapter Six: Eggs— Joan Huff, 24921 Muirlands, No. 205, El Toro, CA 92630; 714/859-3254.

Mod Podge Matte Finish, and small prints for decoupage—PLAID Enterprises, available retail.

White pearls for coach—AK Designs pearls available from Beadiak, 29350 Pacific Coast Hwy, #2A, Malibu, CA 90265, 800/521-2525.

Real goose eggs, filigree and marble base, coach-base and horses, small hinges, and other materials and general information about egg ornamentation—Joan Huff, 24921 Muirlands, No. 205, El Toro, CA 92630; 714/859-3254.

Chapter Seven: Jewelry box—THE BOMBAY COMPANY, P.O. Box 161009, Ft. Worth, TX 76161-1009; 800/829-7789.

Dupioni 100% handwoven silk—LOGANTEX, available retail through the Stitching Corner, 480 Freedom Blvd., Provo, UT 84601; 801/374-1200.

All beads—AK Designs pearls available from Beadiak, 29350 Pacific Coast Hwy, #2A, Malibu, CA 90265, 800/521-2525.

Decorative pin backs—YLI Corporation, P.O. Box 109, Provo, UT 84603, 800/854-1932.

Chapter Eight: For information about silk ribbon embroidery quick-stitched by machine, call the manufacturer or contact your local retailer for the following—Baby Lock (800/422-2952); Pfaff (800/526-0273); and Viking (800/446-2333).

INDEX TO STITCHES

INDEX TO PROJECTS